Har Har Gange

Depiction of Ganga's Descent in Indian Temple Architecture

Rekha Rao

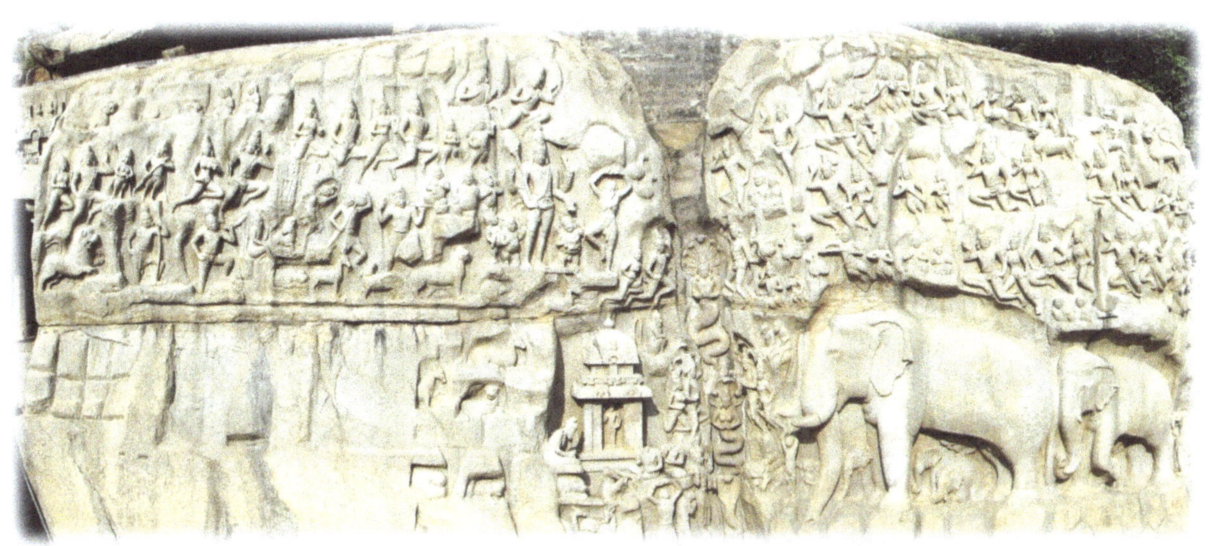

Har Har Gange

Depiction of Ganga's Descent in Indian Temple Architecture

Year of Publication: 2023

© Rekha Rao

This is an intellectual property of the author and cannot be copied or reproduced in any format without the author's permission.

ISBN: 9798867142360

Imprint: Independently published

Table of Contents

Har Har Gange

Depiction of Ganga's Descent in Indian Temple Architecture

River Ganga, nurturing the infinite creatures of creation, is considered the most sacred river and a purifier in Hinduism. She is described in the literary expression of the 108 epithets of Ganga Shata Namavali, the phrases of which are depicted in the temple sculptures. The multiple figures depicting the narrative panels of Gangavatarana, meaning the "descent" of the celestial river Ganga from the heavens to the Earth, are correlated with literary expressions. This profusely illustrative book explores the glorious episode of the Descent of Ganga in the panoramic rock reliefs of Mahabalipuram and the mono-scenic sculptural representations of the different styles of temple architecture of the medieval period. The chant of 'Har Har Gange' associated with the socio-religious rituals associated with the Ganga, unravels Bharat's cultural and spiritual heritage interwoven with the Ganga. This book proves beneficial to art lovers and followers of Hinduism.

I dedicate this book to Bharat, my beloved country.

1. An Introduction to Ganga

Ganga is seen in the physical embodiment of the goddess Ganga/ Ganga Maa in art representations. River Ganga begins its journey from the Gangotri Glacier of the central Himalaya Mountains at Gomukh, the terminus of Gangotri Glacier. When the ice of this glacier melts, it forms the clear waters of river Bhagirati, which joins the Alakananda River as head stream tributaries and officially forms the Ganga River. She flows down as the mighty river through parts of Northern India and drains into the Bay of Bengal. The Ganga River carries nutrient-rich sediment as it flows, depositing fertile soil along its shores. This has allowed civilizations to develop and thrive along the waterway for centuries. The river was used for fishing, irrigation, and bathing and is worshipped in the Hindu religion as Mother Ganga. The river holds immense historical, Puranic, cultural, and religious significance in India and resonates deeply within the hearts of those who encounter its waters. The belief that a dip in its waters can cleanse one's sins and bring spiritual upliftment finds its roots in the early Puranas. The earliest mention of Ganga is in the scriptures of Rigveda 10.75 in the Nadi stuti that quotes – *"Favor ye this land, O Ganga"*…

Emerging from the icy heights of the Himalayas, this sacred river carves its way through the vast plains of India, nurturing and sustaining countless lives along its course.

The story of the descent of the river Ganga by Bhagiratha's efforts can be found in ancient texts such as the Balakanda of Ramayana, Mahabharata, and the Bhagavata Purana. As we navigate the mystical realms surrounding this revered river, we understand why the resounding phrase of "Har Har Gange" echoes through the ages, evoking devotion, and blessings. The phrase comprises three words, and Har is repeated twice with different meanings. Har is an epithet of lord Shiva. The second Har means the captivator of Ganga in his matted locks to prevent its immense flow from flooding the Earth. Though the origin of this slogan is unclear, it has been widely used in religious contexts like the Kumbha mela sung to worship the river Ganga. It has been popular in India's cultural and archaeological contexts for centuries. It is a mantra or slogan that pays homage to the river Ganga and is often recited by devotees together while taking a holy dip in the river.

The introductory part on the Gangavatarana panels elaborates on the significance of three topics:

1.A: The Ganga Stotram.

1.B: The legend of Bhagirata Prayatna followed by Gangavatarana.

1.C: Architectural representations

1.A: The Ganga Stotram

The Ganga Stotram lyrics are beautifully composed to explain the divine nature of Goddess Ganga and the qualities of the river Ganga. Ganga stotra, containing 108 names of Ganga in 14 stanzas, was a simplified version of the initially composed by Adi Shankaracharya's Gangashtaka stotra in the Sanskrit language. (Shankaracharya Krutha Gangashtakam, the octet on Ganga composed by Adi Sankara).

Shankaracharya was a great religious reformer and a pillar of maintaining the original purity of an unparalleled status in the tradition of Advaita Vedanta in Hinduism. Each stanza of the stotra has an in-depth meaning explaining the goddess's divine names and divinity. Some of the Gangavatarana panels may predate the period of Shankaracharya, which means the mythological episode was famous among the followers of Hinduism from early times.

Based on the original version of the Gangashtakam by Adi Shankaracharya, various Hindu texts, poets, and saints have composed their versions of the 108 names of Ganga over time as Ganga Ashtottara ShataNamavali. As for the composer of the Ganga ashtottara Shata Namavali, it is not attributed to a specific composer. The names are part of Hindu religious traditions and have been passed down through generations. Devotees of Ganga recite these names as a form of worship and devotion. The names attributed to Goddess Ganga may vary across different Hindu regions and traditions. The list of 108 names with their number of references has been chosen to compare the literary and archaeological creations. The literary reference Ganga ashtottara Shata Namavali is abbreviated as **GS**, with the phrase number in the text part of the book when referred to. The description of sculptures goes with the names and numbers contained in Ganga ashtottara Shata Namavali. The text of the stotra is provided in the appendix part of this book.

The glorious episode of the descent of the Ganga, her grace, and blessings are described in her 108 epithets. These literary depictions have been correlated in this book with the archaeological representations of Gangadhara panels of Indian temples. The very meaningful phrases of Gangashtaka composed by Adi Shankaracharya is also referred to in this book.

Some names may overlap, while others may be unique to a particular representation. The hymn praises the Goddess of water on how she blesses her devotees, protects and purifies them, and finally leads to Moksha. The meanings involved in each phrase have inspired the sponsors and sculptors who created the panels of this theme. It is believed that once in a lifetime, one must take a holy bath in this river to attain the spiritual essence. At the same time, people firmly believe that immersing the ashes of their kin in the river Ganga helps the spirits to attain moksha.

1.B: The legend of Bhagirata Prayatna followed by Gangavatarana

This chapter delves into the legends and myths that surround the Ganga, revealing the tales of its descent to Earth and the benevolent touch of Lord Shiva, forever intertwining its destiny with the gods. The flow of the river Ganga from heaven to earth (GS.15, *Tri loka patha gamini*) is one of the most popular episodes of Hindu mythology.

The sacred river Ganga is depicted in sculptures in a personified form by the same name. The legend of Ganga in her celestial abode is interesting. Once in the Devaloka, Ganga's upper garment flew due to the breeze, and her breasts were noticed by one of the kings, Mahabhisha, of the Ikshvaku dynasty. Though he was far off, both got attracted to each other. Lord Brahma gets angry over this and curses both to be born as mortals in Bhu loka. Mahabhisha was born as Shantanu. Seeing Ganga in human form, Shantanu gets attracted to and marries her. Ganga destroyed all 7 children born to her; the 8th child was Bhishma. When asked not to destroy the 8th child, she gets angry and returns to her celestial abode. (Adiparva 102-106).

She comes back to Bhuloka again.

According to the legend, King Bhagiratha belonged to the Ikshvaku (Surya Vamsha) dynasty and was an ancestor of King Dasharatha and Sri Rama. Bhagirata's great-grandfather King Sagara of Suryavamsha, an emperor, had conducted the Ashvamedha yaga. The yajna horse was stolen by a demon named Kapila and hidden near sage Kapila's ashram, renowned for its deep meditation and austere practices. King Sagara's three sons, in search of the Aswamedha horse, find it near sage Kapila's Ashram. They wrongly assume it to be sage Kapila's theft, and without paying any respect, they abuse the sage, humiliating him. The curse was inflicted on King Sagara's three sons, which resulted in their headless state and trapped due to their arrogance. (See Fig. 26) Further, all the 60000 sons of King Sagara had been turned to ashes by the sage Kapila's curse for disturbing his penance with noise. The heap of ashes remained with the souls entrapped without any purification rituals. King Sagara's grandsons, Amsumana, and Dilipa performed penance but couldn't achieve the result. After ascending Ayodhya's throne, King Bhagiratha, the grandson of Dilipa, was determined to fulfill the task of his ancestors' salvation. He approaches sage Kapila with devotion to release the state of his forefathers. Sage Kapila guided that the cursed sons of King Sagara could attain salvation only when they were washed in the holy waters of the Ganga. But Ganga resided in the heavens (GS.4 and 5, as *Himachalendra tanaya, and Girimandala gamini,* meaning one who flows in the mountains) and must be brought down to Earth. Bhagiratha, with the guidance of Sage Kapila, embarked on an intense, rigorous penance, praying to the creator of the universe, Lord Brahma, to release Ganga from heaven. Pleased with Bhagiratha's devotion, Lord Brahma granted his wish but cautioned about the immense force involved during the descent of Ganga. Lord Brahma instructed Bhagiratha to pray for Lord Shiva, as only he had the power to withstand the force of Ganga's descent. Bhagiratha prayed accordingly to Lord Shiva and implored him to channel the mighty river as she descended from the heavens to Earth. Upon hearing Bhagiratha's plea, Lord Shiva opened his matted locks and traps the flow of Ganga (GS.19, *Trilochana jata Vasini),* allowing the Ganga to flow through matted locks, skillfully channeling her flow and preventing catastrophic damage.

The torrential flow of Ganga through the Jata of Shiva was still forceful, and she flowed, destroying the farm and Penance of sage Jahnu. Jahnu gets so angry at the damage caused that he consumes the Ganga River in one gulp to teach her a lesson. But the devas and Bhagirata pray to him, telling him about the unliberated status of Bhagirata's forefathers and requesting him to release Ganga. Sage Jahnu then releases Ganga through his ear, and Ganga thus becomes Jahnhavi, the daughter of sage Jahnu.

During her flow, Ganga reaches the ashes of King Sagara's sons and washes over them, granting salvation (GS.7, *Sagaratmaja taraka,* meaning one who liberated the 60000 cursed sons of King Sagara). The sacred river then continued to flow across the Indian subcontinent, giving the fundamental support of water to all living creatures, (GS.43, *Amritakara salila* meaning one whose water is like nectar), purifying the land and blessing all those who came in contact with her waters (GS.51, *Bhagya dayini,* one who brings joy).

1.C: Architectural Representations

Narrative Panels in Stones: The discussion here is to understand variations in the architectural styles of the Bhagirata's penance in the different regions of India. Many temples depicting the story of the descent of Ganga are featured as elaborate narrative panels in temples. These panels are often arranged with many figures sequentially, allowing visitors to follow the storyline while circumambulating the temple.

The narrative panels of the Gangadhara theme are adorned with sculptures of celestial beings, such as Gandharvas, Apsaras, Kinnaras, and Vidhyadharas as side figures along with the main characters like Shiva, Parvati, Ganga, and Bhagiratha. These figures are shown in various poses and engaged in diverse activities, adding a celestial charm to the architecture. Narrative panels are in many varieties.

The rock relief panel of Mahabalipuram belongs to the type of panorama narrative panel. The sculptures often depict mythological stories and religious narratives using space. In narrative panel art, the artist chooses how to portray the story using the space and unfolding the time factor. A panoramic (or panoptic) narrative is a narrative that depicts multiple scenes and actions without the repetition of characters. Actions may be in a sequence or represent simultaneous actions during an event.

The other type is the Mono-scenic narrative, which tells a moment of the story. The panels in temples may be mono-scenic narratives where a story is depicted pictorially without any words. There is no repetition of characters, and only one action is depicted, or it may also depict a sequence of events.

The Grandeur of artistic styles is studied with the representation of ornamentation and religious accessories or motifs. The noticeable variation is the difference in the styles of presenting Shiva, Parvati, and other figures observing the specific way of crown adorning the deity. Makuta means 'Crown' in Sanskrit.

A case study of only the structure of the Makuta, the crown adorning the gods, and its varied representations is considered an example.

Jata Makuta: made of twists of matted hair. Generally worn by Shiva and his class of Gods like Rudra. Brahma is also seen frequently sporting this. This Makuta indicates the Yogic status. For Shiva, in Jata Makuta moon can be on any side, but Sarpa(Snake) is always on the left.

Karanda Makuta means 'Bowl' in Sanskrit. Karanda Makuta is a basket-shaped or bowl-shaped crown with a short height and small size, sometimes depicted on Parvati. Karanda Makuta is a coronet, meaning a small or relatively simple crown, especially worn by lesser royalty and peers or peeresses. Karanda Makuta indicates subordination in status among the pantheon of gods. Usually, female deities or demigods and yakshas are provided with Karanda Makutas. It has three, five, or seven round basket-shaped tiers. The lowest tier is studded with jewels and has a golden band. A Shiikhamani or crest-jewel surmounts the topmost tier. The width of Karanda Makuta should be only one-half or one-third less than that at its base.

Kirita Makuta is a conical or cylindrical crown with a lot of ornamentation and adorned with gemstones of glory. Kirita means' Glory' of royalty. The center of the front side of the crown has a jewel or a central motif. The rest of the crowns are covered with small designs. The crown has the appearance of Taranga (i.e., waves). The base of Kirita Makuta must be curved like an Ardha-Chandra (Crescent shaped) just above the forehead. The height of the Kirita Makuta should be two or three times the length of the wearer's face. It symbolizes the superior nature of the wearer, and he has many subordinates to do his work. Parvati and Shiva's figures also show Kiritamakuta in front, along with Jatamakuta. Kirita Makuta can be worn by Chkrakavarthis, who conquered beyond seas.

The skills in architectural creations, though conceptualized in the frame of religious and art prescriptions, the sculptor's imaginations were based on the literary sources that inspired them a lot in making these panels attractive.

The Rock relief architecture of Mahabalipuram is very elaborate and depicts the story of Bhagirata's penance. Hence, the discussion of over 100 figures makes the discussion elaborate. It is more straightforward in the other temples and does not cover the complete legend part.

The terms "Gangavatarana" (Ganga + avatarana, meaning the descent from top to down), Gangadhara (The wearer of Ganga on the headdress), or Bhagirata prayatna (Bhagirata's efforts) have been used for Shiva in this book.

These panels, though depict the same theme, belong to different times and have exciting and varied presentations like a tableau in the stone medium. The episode of Gangavatarana is depicted in many temples in India. In this book, only four architectural styles of varying periods are discussed. They are:

1. The representations of the Pallava style of architecture belonging to the 7th Century CE, in the Granite stones, Mahabalipuram, Tamil Nadu.Two more representations of Gangadhara Shiva from Kailasanathar temple at Kancheepuram in the Pallava style are discussed.

2. Early Chalukya style, of the 6th Cen. CE, built in the Sandstone of Aihole, Karnataka.

3. Two panels in the Rashtrakuta style, are analyzed here, which were built between the 5th and 8th centuries CE by cutting the high basalt steep rock walls. They are Elephanta Cave No 1, in Maharashtra, and the Kailasaa Ellora caves (Cave No. 16), also in Maharashtra.

4. Two panels of Chola-style of art in granite stone at the Ekambareshwara temple, Tamil Nadu, of the 7th Cen. CE. is discussed in this book.

All four monuments are inscribed on India's UNESCO World Heritage Sites for their architectural and historical grandeur.

The intention of the analysis also involves the different ways in which the figure of Parvati is depicted. Gangadhara remains the same as the very heroic figure stretching his matted hair. But Parvati, though looking very graceful, is depicted with astonishment in some, with a fearful expression in some figures and a smiling figure showing her admiration for Shiva, who could easily handle the force of Ganga.

The abbreviations used in this book are:

GS - Ganga ashtottara Shatanamavali;

LR panel – Low relief panel;

HR panel - High-relief panel

2. Gangavataranana in Pallava Style at Mamallapuram

Mamallapuram, now called Mahabalipuram, is in Chengalpattu district Tamil Nadu, lying at the shore of the Bay of Bengal, and is an ancient historical town. It has some best examples of the age-old monolithic rock-cut architecture of the 7th Century CE, especially during the reign of the great Pallava King Mahendravarman I, also known as "Mamalla", the Great Warrior.

These monuments are now a part of the UNESCO World Heritage sites, providing excellent exposure to the Pallava Art. Mamallapuram (also now known as Mahabalipuram), in southeast India, has a particular monolithic rock relief depicting a spiritual theme of the "The descent of Ganga" the tableau of the auspicious moment. This sculptured rock incorporates religious storytelling, including over one hundred depictions of humans, deities, and animals in joyful scenes eagerly waiting to see Ganga's descent. The Ganga is *"Triloka patha Gamini"*, (GS,15), the only river that flows from all three worlds: The heaven/swarga, the Earth/Bhuloka, and Patala/the underground.

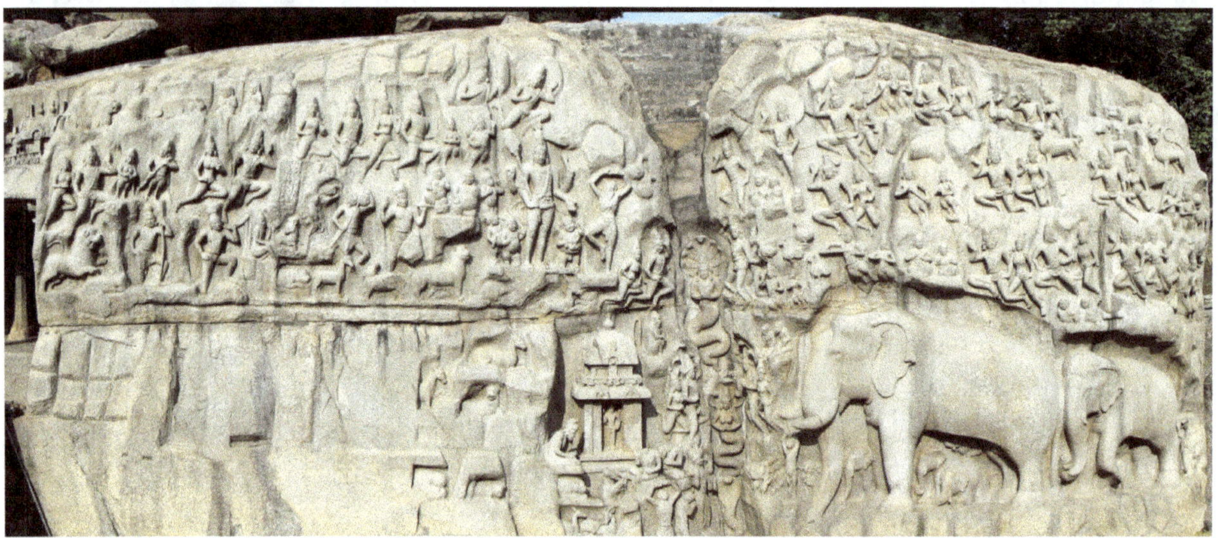

Fig. 1: The High relief rock panel (HR panel)

It is the most well-known of the monuments at Mamallapuram, carved from a massive monolithic granite boulder. It is one of the most enormous relief sculptures in the world. The rock measures around 96 by 43 feet (29 m × 13 m), in height and length. The rock relief dates to the 7th -8th century during the reign of the Pallava dynasty. The carvings on the rock cover most of the faces of two adjoining boulders, with a large cleft in the center. The Descent of Ganga, also known as the Bhagiratha episode, is a significant event in Hindu mythology. It tells the story of King Bhagiratha's efforts to bring the sacred river Ganga from the heavens to Earth.

Near this boulder is one more monolithic carving with almost the same theme in Mahabalipuram. The rock, slightly smaller in structure, appears to be created earlier, and the more extensive work was done with the same theme but with better clarity and workmanship. However, both rock relief works appear unfinished, as many parts are marked but left uncarved.

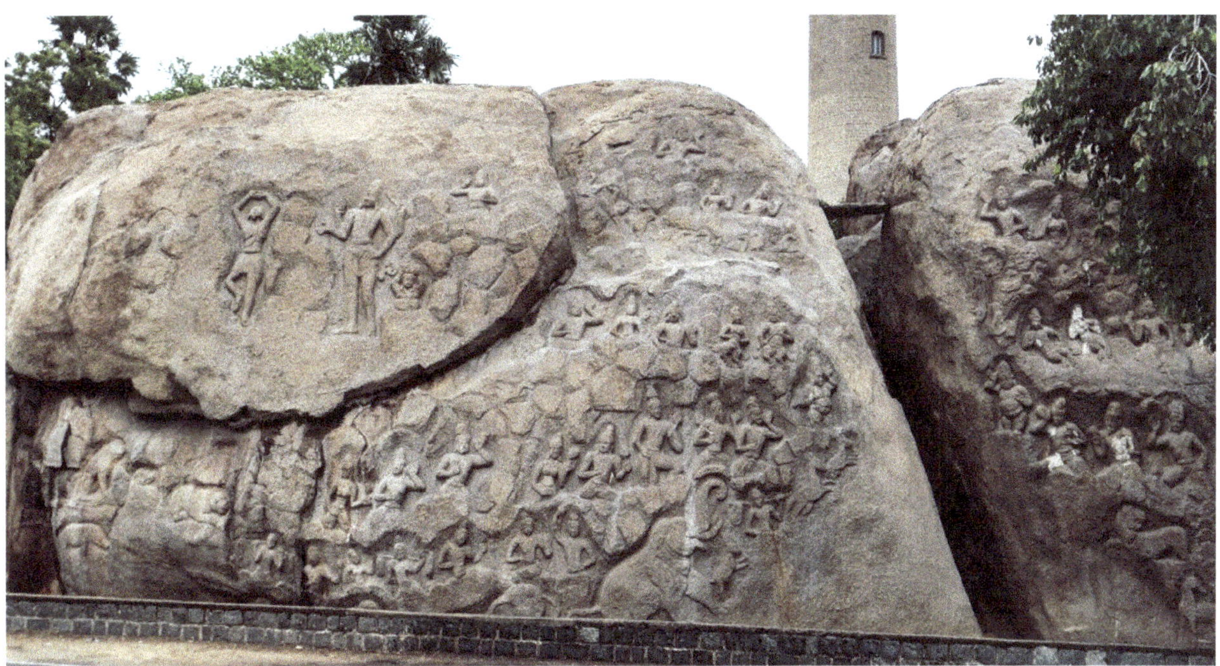

Fig. 2: The low-relief rock panel (LR Panel)

Despite its long history of at least 1,200 years and plenty of scholarly attention, experts remain uncertain about its precise subject matter of recreation. The reason for making two rock carvings with almost the same theme is the precise subject matter of the enigmatic artwork. Though both structures have the same story base, the story part occupies a small area, and the descriptive central part involves figures of flying demigods, many humans, and wild animals.

This chapter focuses on why two boulders were planned with a similar theme. Why are so many animals and gods all put together, and all are moving towards the cleft than seeing the figure of Shiva?

The Pallava king created the religious story in rock relief work in Mamallapuram, commemorating their victory over Chalukyas. It is now a part of the UNESCO World Heritage sites, providing excellent exposure to the Pallava Art.

The discussion in this article proceeds with more information in the sub-chapters as follows:

2.A: A brief historical account of the sponsor of this work.

2.B: The geology of the rocks at Mamallapuram.

2.C: A general overview of rock relief art in architecture.

2.D: Recognizing the deeper layers of meaning.

2.E: Recreation of the descent of ganga in Mamallapuram panel.

2.F: The three lokas of the universe.

2.G: The upper zone of immortals: Swargaloka as depicted in the relief art.

2.H: The mid-zone: Bhuvar loka/Antariksha.

2.I: Earth zone: Bhu loka of mortals.

2.J: The underground Patala loka.

2.K: Gangadhara Shiva panels from the Kailasanathar temple at Kancheepuram.

2.A: A brief historical account of the sponsor of this work

The Pallavas a South Indian dynasty, rose to power after the decline of the Gupta dynasty. In The early medieval period, the region that is present-day Tamil Nadu in South India was known as "Tamilakam" or "Tamilaham," which translates to "the land of Tamils. It was ruled by various political dynasties entities, such as the Cholas, Pandyas, and Pallavas, who ruled over different parts of the region at different times. The earliest known Pallava ruler was Simhavarman I, who ascended the throne around the 3rd century CE. However, it was under the reign of his successors, particularly Mahendravarman I (600-630 CE) and Narasimhavarman I (630-668 CE), that the Pallavas reached the zenith of their power and influence, which was called the Golden Age of Pallavas.

Pallavas were worshippers of Shiva and were known for constructing many monolithic shrines of Dravidian style, significantly contributing to the region's art, architecture, and culture. Their distinctive architectural style influenced later dynasties in South India.

The rock relief carving of "Gangavatarana" – the "Descent of the Ganga" as it is popularly called is a complex and intricate composition showcasing the Pallava dynasty's artistic and sculptural prowess. The relief was created during the reign of King Narasimhavarman I also known as Mamalla, and hence the place was called Mamallapuram. Pallava dynasty under Narasimhavarman I emerged as a major power in South India, marking the beginning of a golden age of the history and culture of the Pallava dynasty.

He aspired to celebrate his victory over the Chalukya king Pulakesin II. Narasimhavarman I was considered one of the most prominent kings of the Pallava dynasty, which peaked in the seventh and eighth centuries C.E. He sponsored the construction of magnificent rock-cut temples and monolithic rathas (chariots) at Mamallapuram, which are impressive examples of Pallava architecture today. He patronized art, architecture, and literature, and his reign saw the artistic and cultural activities flourishing well.

The Pallavas were great art patrons, and their sculptures often incorporated religious and secular themes. The "Descent of the Ganga" is a testament to their skill and creativity, depicting the mythological narrative and scenes from everyday life, such as animals, hunters, hermits, and celestial musicians.

The Pallavas' fascination with the descent of the Ganga episode can be attributed to several factors.

Firstly, it allowed them to showcase their devotion to Hindu deities, particularly Lord Shiva, who played a significant role in the episode. The episode provided them with a rich artistic and narrative subject matter for their architectural and sculptural creations, allowing them to demonstrate their artistic prowess.

Secondly, The Chalukya and Pallava dynasties frequently clashed over territorial disputes, control of trade routes, and political influence in the region. The victory of the Pallava king Narasimhavarman in releasing his territory from the clutches of early Chalukyas and Cholas was probably paralleled to Bhagirata's efforts.

Lastly, Pallava kings recreated this important religious story for onlookers and dignitaries commemorating a victory. The Pallavas controlled the Kaveri, a significant river source of regional political strength. The rulers probably wanted to connect the Kaveri and the Ganga symbolically to remind viewers of their earthly and divine power. The river Ganga held immense religious significance for Hindus, symbolizing purity, divinity, and salvation. The waters of the Ganga were believed to possess supernatural powers. By incorporating this episode into their artistic and architectural endeavors, the Pallavas could evoke a sense of religious sanctity and connect with the larger Hindu community, connecting with the broader Hindu tradition of post-death rituals of releasing the ashes of the deceased fathers in river/sea waters.

2.B: The geology of the rocks at Mamallapuram

Mamallapuram is famous for its giant open-air rock relief, which is the focus of this article. The rock-cut architecture is a type of Rock Art in which a structure is created by carving it out of solid natural rock. The rock on which the Descent of the Ganga is carved in rock relief faces East. It is primarily a pink granite stone.

The geological formations of granites in Mamallapuram resulted from the ancient geological processes of several episodes of tectonic activity, including volcanic activity that took place over millions of years. These geological processes led to the formation of the granites and Charnockites prominent in and around Mamallapuram. Boulders are naturally scattered throughout the region, and there are over one hundred of these in situ carvings. Many monolithic rocks are in Mamallapuram with a natural cleavage in the middle. Some developed a wider gap, while some had a narrow cleft.

Mahabalipuram region has two types of rocks: 1) Granite and 2) Charckonite. The two rock relief boulders chosen for this study have a cleft in between that is naturally formed. Mamallapuram's granite rock belt was primarily igneous rock formed by the cooling of magma near the earth's surface.

Granite is an intrusive igneous rock formed from the slow cooling process of magma deep within the Earth's crust. It is a coarse-grained rock comprising minerals such as quartz, feldspar, and mica. The reason for this cleft formation was that the monolithic granite rock boulders split due to varied natural forces making horizontal or vertical cracks due to extreme heat and pressure and getting rounded off with time. Many rocks in the Mamallapuram area have huge slits, as shown in Fig.3 (1-7).

These stones are known for their durability, and the intricate rock-cut sculptures have withstood the test of time. The artisans of the Pallava times took advantage of the natural properties of granite to create impressive and long-lasting works of art, and they excelled in rock relief architecture. The granite rock belt in Mamallapuram is famous for its monolithic structures.

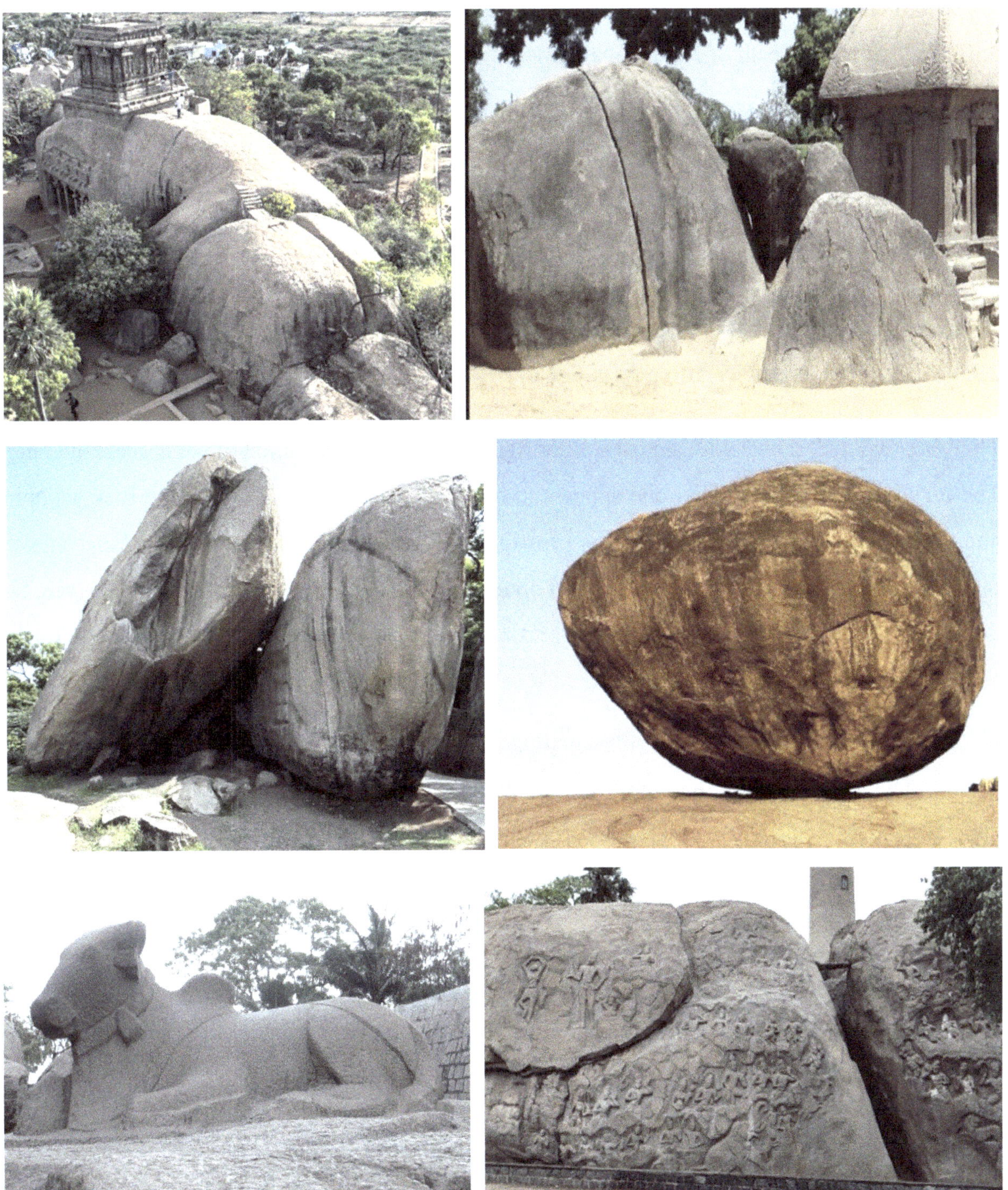

Fig. 3: (A-F) Rocks with a natural cleave in Mamallapuram

The Pancha Rathas (temples in the form of chariots), the rock-cut cave, and the rock relief works were carved out of giant granite boulders in the 7th and 8th centuries. The monuments are mostly cut along the faces of a cliff and are monolithic, carved out of a single piece in situ granite. The intricately designed edifices represent the early stages of Dravidian architecture in the Rathas.

These structures were never consecrated because they were never completed and were left unfinished after the death of Narasimhavarman.

Charnockite: Charnockite is another rock type of granitic rock, typically medium to coarse-grained, found in the Mahabalipuram area. Charnockite rocks are known for their durability, making them suitable for architectural purposes. Many ancient temples, the shore temple, and monuments in Mahabalipuram were constructed using Charnockite. The Charnockites are the strongest and the most durable rock yet quite responsive to fine dressing.

2.C: A general overview of rock relief art

There are two rock reliefs with almost similar figures and theme execution of the descent of Ganga. The earlier and slightly smaller one appears to be a trial work as it looks crude in rock scooping and unfinished. The earlier version was probably not satisfactory for the Pallava king, and the theme was repeated on a slightly more giant boulder with a naturally formed cleft in between, like the earlier trial one. Alternately, King had encouraged the younger sculptors to practice and learn rock-cutting techniques on a giant boulder.

Rock relief architecture in India is a fascinating aspect of the country's rich architectural heritage. Rock reliefs are large-scale sculptures carved directly into natural rock formations or artificially created rock surfaces. These reliefs often depict religious, mythological, or historical subjects and represent meaningful artistic and cultural representations. The theme of the Decent of Ganga is carved in two giant monolithic granites at Mamallapuram with naturally formed fissures in them.

Relief in architecture is a sculptural method in which many sculptures project or are raised from a supporting plane base. The figures remain attached to a solid background of the same material.

Rock relief art comes in two varieties:

1. Bas or low relief type where the sculptures project only slightly from the background giving a 2D figure.

2. A high or great relief where the forms of the figures stand out. They are projected at least half or more of their natural circumference from the background giving the visual effect of a 3D figure to a certain extent.

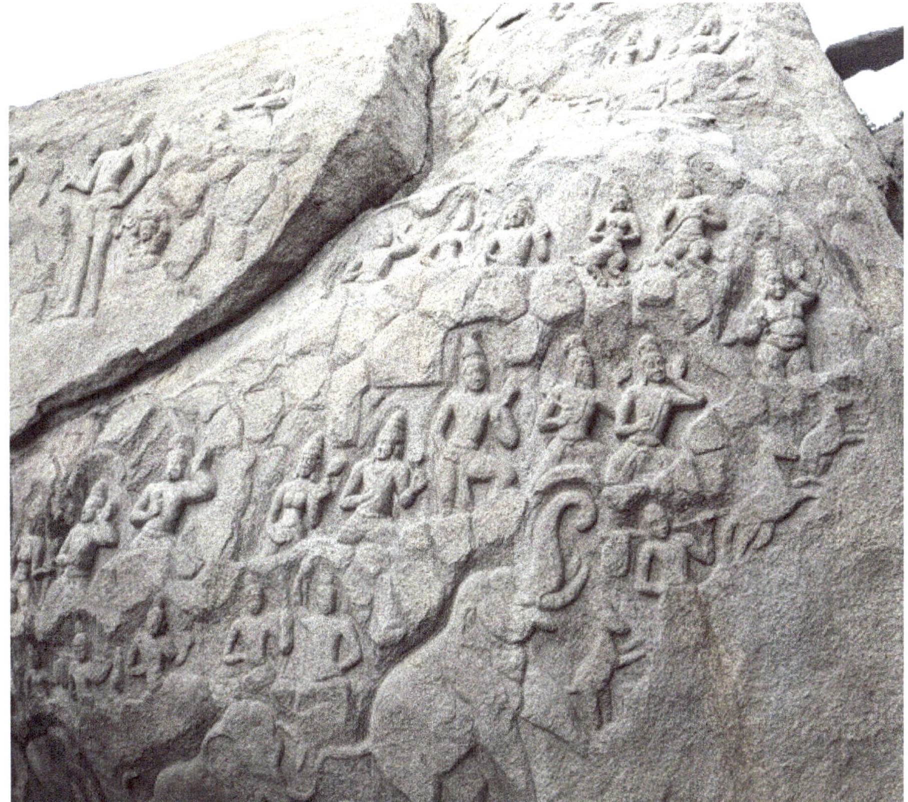

Fig. 4: Earlier rock carving in low relief (LR) panel

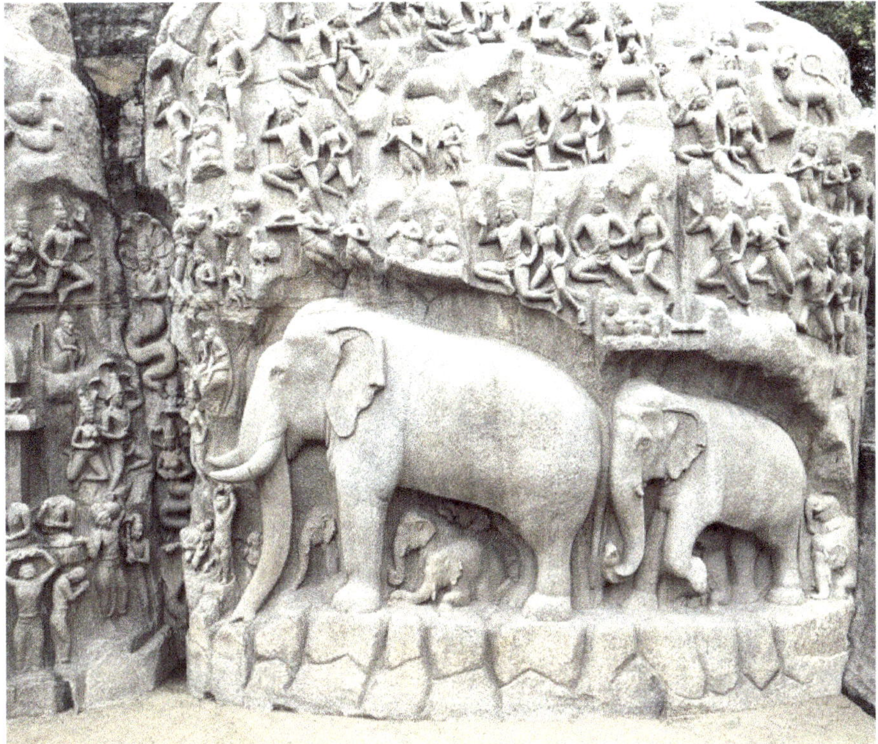

Fig. 5: Later Recreated rock carving in high relief (HR) panel

The two reliefs are differentiated in this article as LR (Low relief, the earlier version) and HR (High relief and the latter version) panels. They are studied comparatively to understand why two rock relief works were done with the same theme. Though beautiful, the earlier LR panel is neglected, and the HR panel is maintained well. The exploration of over a hundred figures commences by examining the deep spiritual connections Ganga holds within the tapestry of Hinduism.

In a general overview of how rock relief art is typically done, the first step in creating rock relief art is choosing a large rock surface with a suitable texture for carving. The rock surface was usually prepared by cleaning dirt or loose debris and treated to enhance its durability and longevity. According to the theme, a detailed blueprint of the intended artwork was done. Different tools and techniques were employed to transfer the design to the rock surface before carving the rock relief. The sculptor then works systematically from larger to more minor details, gradually removing layers of rock material to create the desired depth and shape. The process requires skill, precision, and a deep understanding of the rock's properties to avoid accidental damage. The artist refines the relief's details by smoothing rough edges, adding intricate features, and polishing it finally with sandpaper to achieve the desired texture and finish on rock relief art. Protective coatings will be applied to maintain the rock surface clean. The relief art has withstood the test of time, the salty sea breeze, and the weather extremes for over thirteen centuries and still looks magnificent.

2.D: Recognizing the deeper layers of meaning

Both panels portray the story of King Bhagiratha's penance and the descent of the river Ganga from the heavens. It is a stone carving masterpiece, showcasing the ancient sculptors' incredible skill and artistry. The details and intricacies of the panel are awe-inspiring.

Through the theme of descent of Ganga, the LR and HR panels have also focused on the core Vedic theme of creation, "Vasudhaiva Kutumbakam," which can be translated as "the world is one family." It is an ancient Indian concept, a Sanskrit phrase from the Maha Upanishad. This phrase, a philosophical teaching in Hinduism, reflects the idea of the interconnectedness of all animals, human beings, and divines.

All figures in both panels depict movement and activity. There is no marked difference in physical form between the divines, Semi-divines, and the earthly man or woman. The entire creation of two-legged ones, all the avian birds, all types of four-legged animal creations, amphibians, snakes, and the lords of the underworld without feet are all in one rock and exist to be in harmony. All forms of life were overwhelmed that the celestial river Ganga, whose water is as precious as life-giving Amrita, (GS. 43, *Amritakara salila*, meaning whose water is like nectar) was to reach the land from great heights. All figures in both panels focus on the cleft and show eagerness to see the tremendous one-time event of the descent of Ganga. The imagination and technique of the skilled Pallava sculptors to create the episode without giving any personified representation of Ganga has no match. Water stored on the top part of the rock was designed to fall in the cleft to create the effect of the water falling.

Adi Shankaracharya has used the phrase to describe the forceful descent of Ganga to "*Brahmandam Khandayanti*"meaning Breaking the universe into two.

"Khallorkat Apatanti Kanakagiri guha ganda shailat skhalanti" meaning falling from the heights of heaven, falling torrentially on earth.

This expression of Gangastaka can be correlated with the huge rock of Mahabalipuram and the natural slit it has is utilized to make the phrase "Brahmandam *Khandayanti*" more pictorial.

Why were all earth creatures waiting to witness the celestial singular event?

In philosophy, "singular event" or "unique event" is often used to describe a one-time event. A singular event is an occurrence that happens only once and does not repeat or have similar instances. This term emphasizes the exceptional and non-recurring nature of the event, highlighting its distinctiveness and individuality within a larger context.

Water is the essence of life required by all creatures on Earth. All creatures have been delighted and eager to witness the flow of the river Ganga and participate in the one-time event, becoming an eternal phenomenon.

Elephants are essential in both panels because they are central to the defense forces. All kings had elephants in great numbers. Elephants were large-bodied and required rivers for their survival.

Nagas from the underground loka have come up to welcome and witness the flow of Ganga with folded hands.

Fig. 5 looks like a depiction of the three worlds. Patala by the Naga couple, Bhu loka with men and animals, many Gandharva and Kinnara couples, Sadhyas or Rishis in the mid zone, and the upper svarga loka with deities with a significant halo.

The picture shows many wild animals hiding in a cave, like lions and lionesses. The heard of elephants, deer, ducks, peacocks, langur monkeys, rabbits, boar, tortoise, and a monitor lizard all are depicted on the rock. Hunters are there carrying the animal gives a perfect picture of the forest scene.

Many scholars have called the relief related to Arjuna's penance and Lord Shiva holding the Pashupatastra in his right hand and offering it to Arjuna as a boon in Varada hasta. It is tough to find convincing logic as there is no proof in sculptures supporting the Kiratarjuneya episode. Neither Shiva nor Arjuna is depicted as hunters, nor the carcass of a wild boar that was hunted is depicted on the rock. The panorama of all semi-divines and earthly beings is not part of the episode of Arjuna's penance. The rock relief designed with the natural cleft to the fall of water is not connected to Arjuna's penance or the Kirartarjuniya, a famous episode of Mahabharata.

On the other hand, Bhagiratha belonged to the solar Ikshvaku dynasty of the lineage of Sri Rama and Dasharatha. Bhagiratha was the grandson of King Sagara's son Dilipa.

Lord Hanuman, an immortal being according to Hindu mythology was a celestial being and an incarnation of Lord Shiva's divine energy (Marked with an arrow in Fig.6). Hanuman holds a half-moon-shaped object in his left hand. As per Hindu mythology - The Ramayana, Lord Hanuman was a member of the Vanar (half man-half monkey) tribe and reincarnation of Lord Shiva. He was a superhero because of his majestic powers, and he played a crucial role in the Ramayana. The crescent moon may be a symbolic representation of some values, like the ethereal zone (abode of the moon) carried in his left hand.

He is believed to be present on earth and has been represented in the HR panel to remind about his association with the Ikshvaku dynasty lineage. It is believed that Hanuman assumed a nano form after the death of Sri Rama and went straight to the Nag Loka, the world of serpent king Vasuki. Many Vanaras are depicted gazing at the crack from where the serpent deities are arising as though they are waiting to see Hanuman and the waterfall. (See Fig 7, marked with arrows). Fig.8 shows an ordinary monkey's activity of searching for lice, and these monkeys look different from the ones in Fig. 6 and 7.

Hanuman's power of transcending the boundaries of time and mortality is in many representations of monkeys, like the associates of Hanuman, and monkeys in their usual activity in the current period. These depictions support tracing the theme of rock relief associated with Bhagirata's penance, an episode of Ramayana, and unrelated to Arjuna's penance.

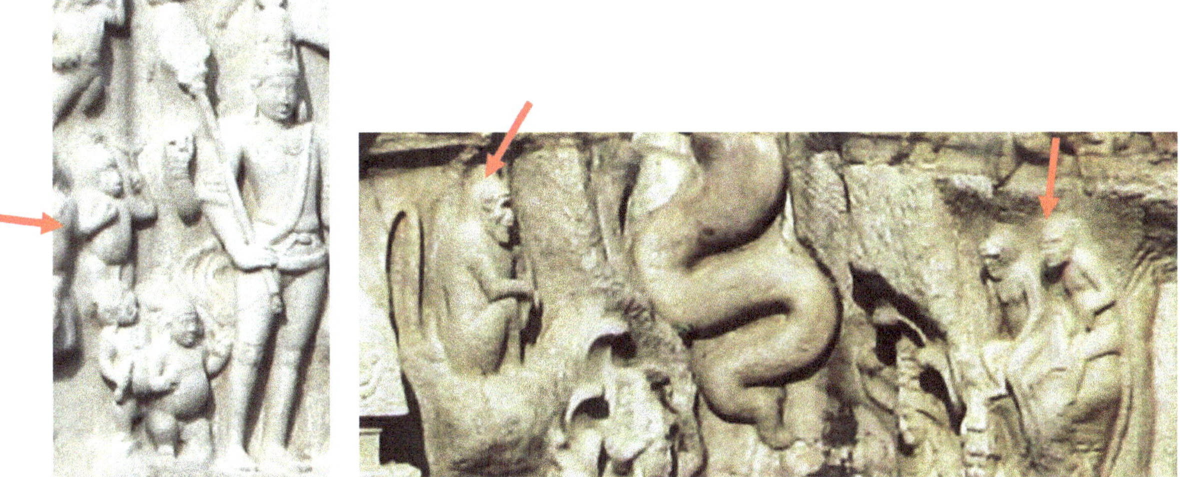

Fig. 6 (Left) and Fig. 7 (Right): Depiction of Vanaras in the HR panel

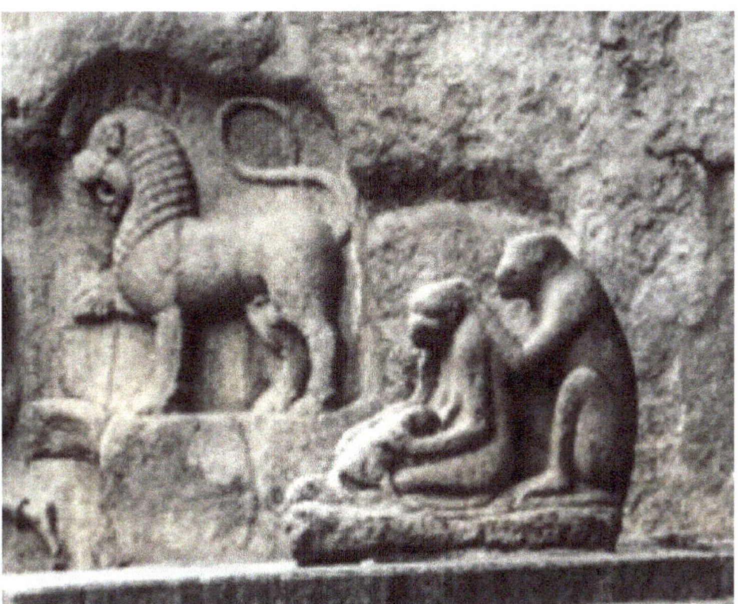

Fig. 8: Monkeys depicted in their usual activities

2.E: Re-creation of the descent of Ganga

The reasons for re-creating the rock relief, the Descent of Ganga theme could be as follows:

1) The figures on the LR panel in low relief with a slight projection of figures were less imposing.

2) The HR panel was made with higher relief work with a more excellent projection of figures, almost like 3D figures (Fig. 9 and 10).

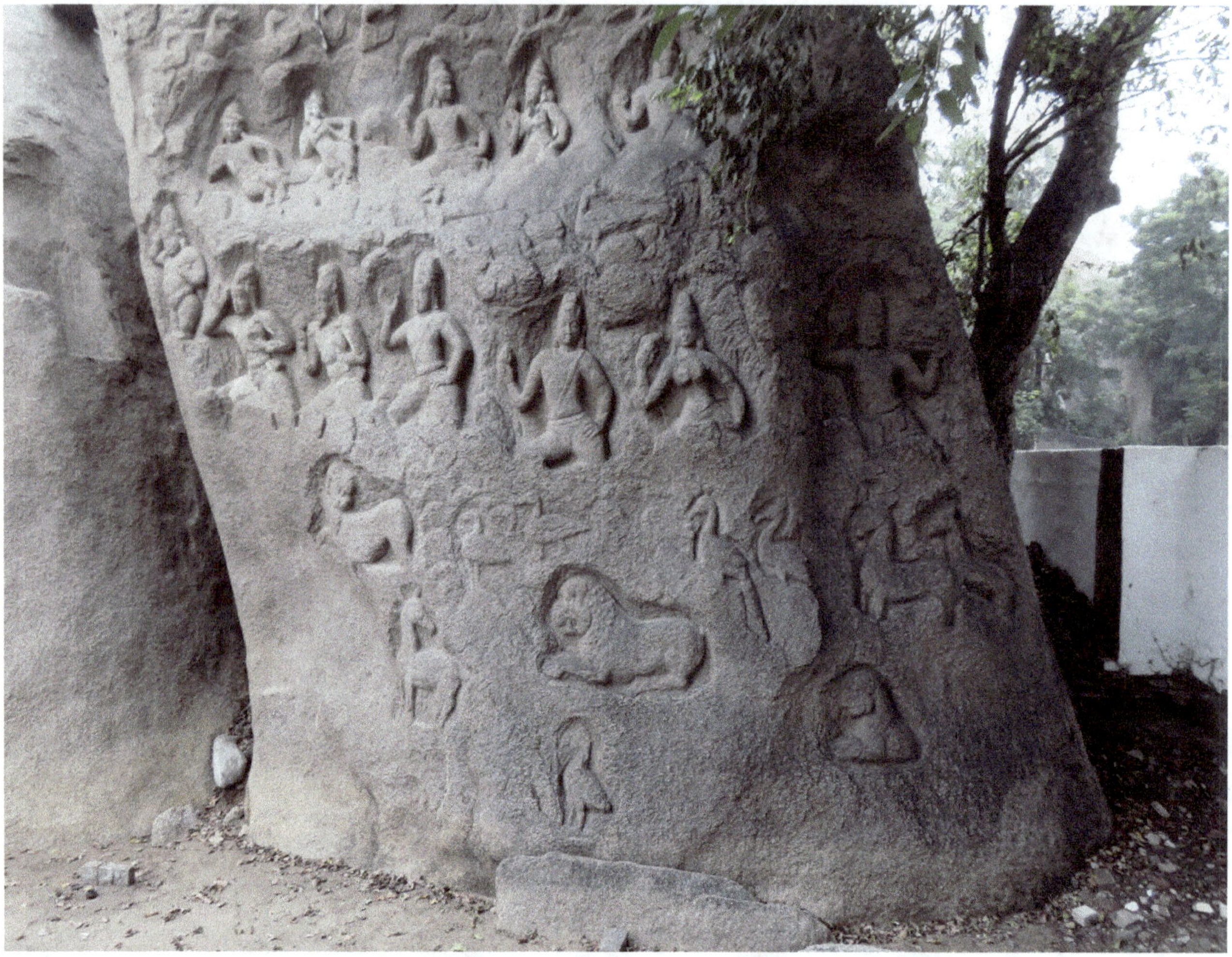

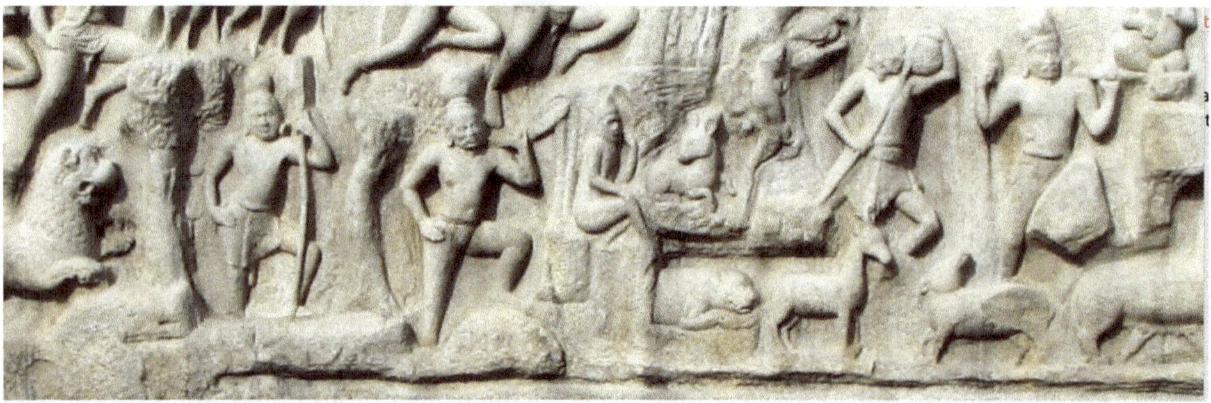

Fig. 9: Depiction of animals in the LR panel

Fig. 10: Depiction of animals and men in the HR panels

This redefining of the theme called for more significant experience and skills in artists to create high-relief figures. Probably skilled artists were willing to create a High-relief carving as it was with an enhanced visual effect compared to Low-relief carvings. Much of the rock surface on the LR panel was blank without utilizing the space. This aspect is also redesigned in the HR panel. The animals, like deer and birds, are drawn around the lion in the LR panel, and much of the space is not utilized. The rock carving looks crude compared to the high-relief work.

Many figures of flying gods in the LR panel are only with the torso (Fig. 9), and the leg part was not defined. Even the figures of animals like elephants, deer, or goats are without the complete leg part. This has been refined in the HR panel. (Fig. 10)

The figures in both panels are slender and delicately made with a smiling face. It gives a pleasant picture of how the world consists of divines, men, animals, and birds, all as part of creation. Even animals show their emotions, a great artistic skill of the sculptors of the Pallava period. Probably the artists who worked on the HR panel were different from those who tried the LR panel.

The blueprint of the LR panel was probably found lacking clarity as the core theme figures of Shiva and Bhagirata . They are on a separate part in a corner and do not gel with the theme of the descent of Ganga. This aspect seems to have been corrected in the HR panel by placing Shiva and Bhagirata near the fall of water.

2.F: The zones of the Universe

The Vedas, the oldest sacred texts of Hinduism, do not explicitly mention three separate worlds. However, they do describe different realms or planes of existence. These realms Heaven, Earth, and Atmosphere in between are often called "loka" in Sanskrit. In Hindu cosmology, the universe is divided into three significant realms. They are:

Bhu Loka: Also known as the Earthly or the physical realm of mortals, is where the world men inhabit. The physical plane of existence includes the material universe and all living beings on Earth.

Bhuvar Loka: Bhuvar Loka is often described as the intermediary between earth and heaven, the celestial realms, or the astral plane. It is associated with celestial bodies, including the sun, moon, stars, planets, and the flying semi-divines in a personified form.

Swarga Loka: It is considered heaven, the abode of light, divine bliss, and enjoyment. According to Vedic traditions, it is inhabited by gods, immortals, and righteous souls who have performed exemplary deeds in their earthly lives.

Patala Loka: Patala refers to the netherworld or the subterranean realms below the Earth's surface which are seven. Vedas do not mention Patala, it is extensively described in the Puranas, Brahmanas, and Upanishads, which explore philosophical and cosmological themes. Patala is said to be located beneath the Earth and is described as a vast and complex realm with multiple levels or layers. It is inhabited by various beings, including Nagas (many serpent-like creatures in Mahatala), and Danavas (demons in Rasatala loka) believed to be the abode of several powerful demons and occasionally serves as the setting for various mythological events and battles between gods and demons and other supernatural entities. Patala is often portrayed as a dark and mysterious underworld, contrasting with the heavenly realms above. In Hindu mythology, Patala is sometimes associated with the serpent deity Vasuki, who is said to reside there with other serpents.

Creatures from all three worlds and Patala Loka were eagerly waiting to witness the spectacular view of the descent of Ganga.

2.G: The upper zone of immortals: Swargaloka

A row of swans in the top level of the LR panel gives a picture of the Swargaloka, which defines the abode of Gods. It gives a picture of Shiva and Parvati whose abode is Mount Kailasa. (See Fig. 11). Hamsa represents the sacred symbol of the soul, symbolically displaying the ascent of spiritual purity levels. One of the names of Ganga (GS.62 is *Hamsa Svarupini*-meaning a personification of flying divine swans. Ganga is compared to the swans which fly around the mountains, and Ganga flows through the mountains. (GS. 5 *Girimandala meaning* one who flows through the mountains and Naga putrika, (GS.26, daughter of the mountain., Naga means mountain) and also, the one who is leaping over mountains (GS.44. *Lila lamghita parvata*). Below the birds in Fig. 11 are seen the rocks of mountains.

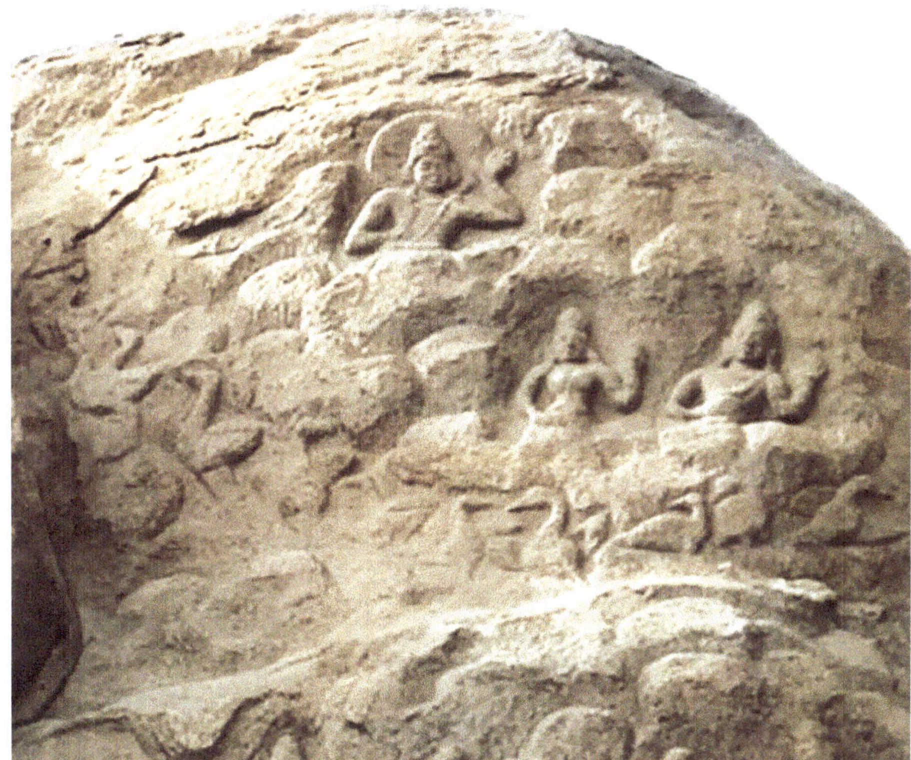

Fig. 11: The row of swans defining the abode of Gods, the Swargaloka

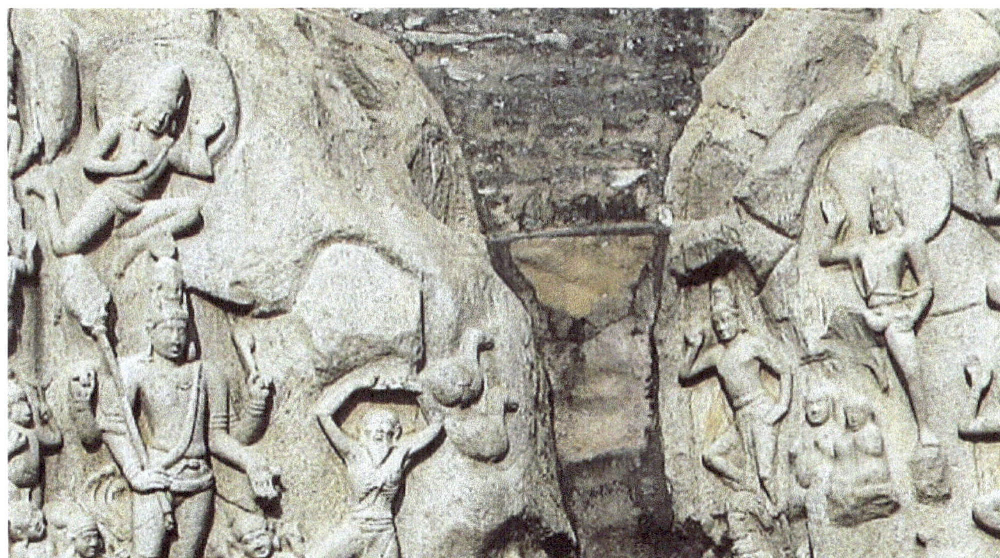

Fig. 12: Depiction of the moon god above Shiva, the Sun god on the opposite side, and birds defining the abode of Gods

The zone of Swargaloka, the abode of Gods, is not well defined in the HR panel. Only two ducks are indicated near Bhagirata's hand. In the HR panel, the Sun and Moon Gods are in personified forms in the top row, depicted with a big halo that defines the upper zone. They are waiting to welcome the descent of Ganga from their abode of the upper world to the lower zone of the earth.

The figure of Bhagirata:

In both panels, King Bhagirata, wearing a short costume, is in rigorous penance and is depicted almost similarly in both panels with one leg raised and hands lifted in a Hatha yoga posture. Shiva is four-armed in both panels.

Shiva in Fig 13 is four-armed, without many ornaments. His right hand seems to be a gesture of what Bhagirata wants as a boon. In the backhand holds a small Damaru and a club. He shows Katyavalambita mudra (Hand resting on the lower waist). Shiva is not depicted in the LR panel with his open Jata to restrict the force of the fall of Ganga, nor is there a representation of Ganga in a personified or perceived form.

In the LR panel, the figure of a short and stout Gana carrying food on the head is seated by the side of Shiva. Parvati is not depicted.

Bhagirata is the emaciated figure in a Hatha yoga posture of standing on one leg with raised hands in penance.

Shiva, in Fig. 14, the HR panel, is the most prominent figure granting the boon in Varada hasta of granting a boon. He holds a long vale (a lancet / shula) in his right hand and left hand in a giving gesture. Both the back arms are folded at shoulder level, and in Kapittha hand gesture holds the thin strand of his jata to arrest the flow of Ganga. 3-4 figures of short and stout ganas are at Shiva's knee level. One Gana is depicted with a lion's face in the belly.Parvati is not depicted here.

Bhagirata is in a Hathayoga posture of balancing on one leg with raised hands in penance.

Ganga is not depicted in a personified form in both panels. Her flow is expected to be visualized as water flow in the cleft. In the HR panel, Both Shiva and Bhagiratha in penance, are depicted close to the cleft where Ganga was to descend. She is in an unmanifest form denoting in Prakriti form on account of the subtleness of its nature.She is *Avyakta* (GS. 35, meaning unmanifest). The fall of water as a continued part of Bhagiratha's penance is left to the viewers' imagination. Her fall and flow are understandable only through the artistic subtle activity of other creatures. She is seen as *Jalarupa,* the divine form of water (GS.96).

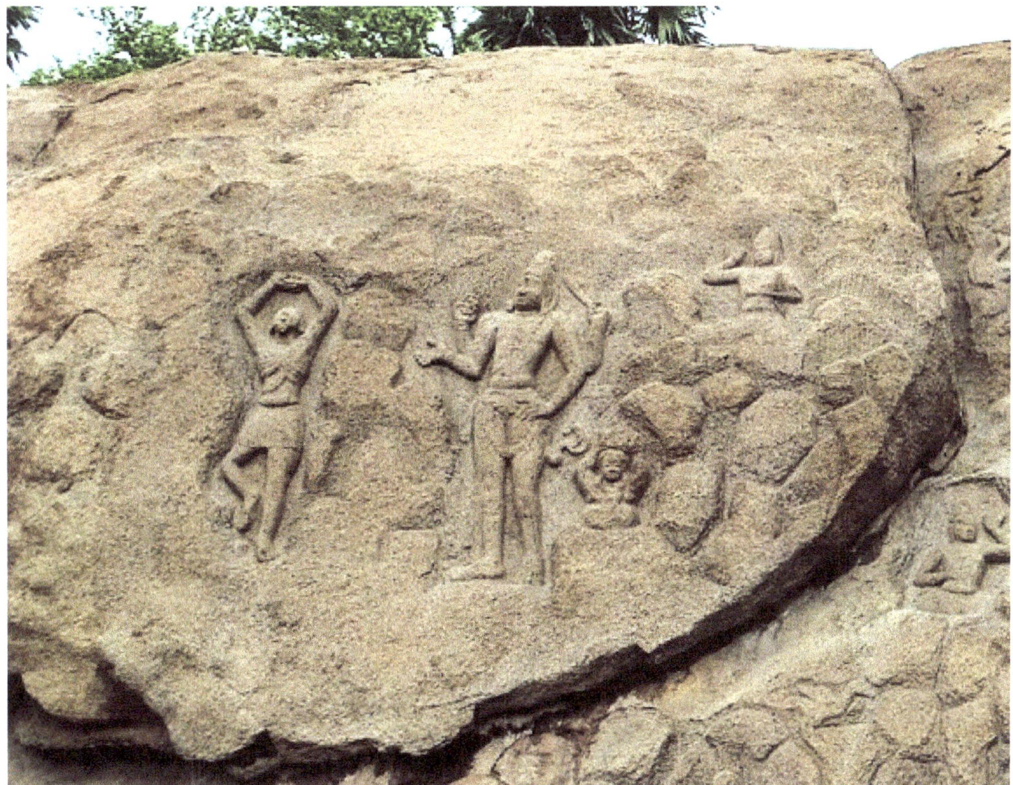

Fig. 13: LR Panel of Bhagirata's penance and Lord Shiva granting the boon

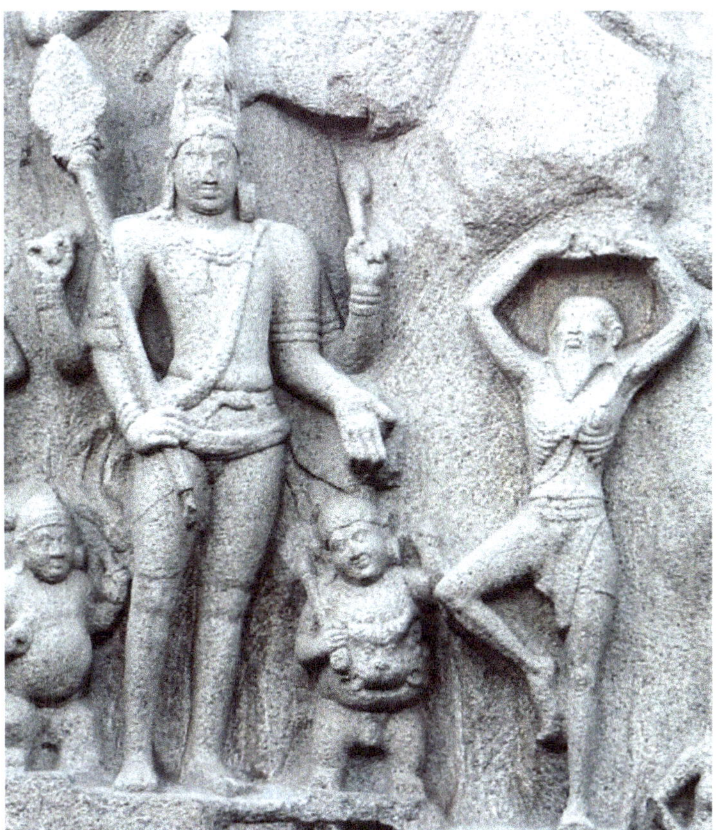

Fig. 14: *HR Panel of Bhagirata's penance and Lord Shiva granting the boon*

2.H: The mid-zone: Bhuvar Loka / Antariksha

According to Hindu cosmology, Bhuvar loka is the second zone of atmosphere between the Sun (sky), and the earthly physical world, inhabited by semi-divines.

Many mystic figures of the flying semi-divine gods hover in mid-air, and the atmosphere is depicted to indicate the abode of Bhuvar loka. All figures depict their eagerness to see Ganga because she is Nandinyai (GS.52) pleasing to one's eyes and delightful. She is also *Nayanaananda daayini* and *Ramya* (GS.25 and 33, meaning pleasant to the eyes and beautiful). Ganga is also described as *Sarvadeva svaroopini* (GS.105).

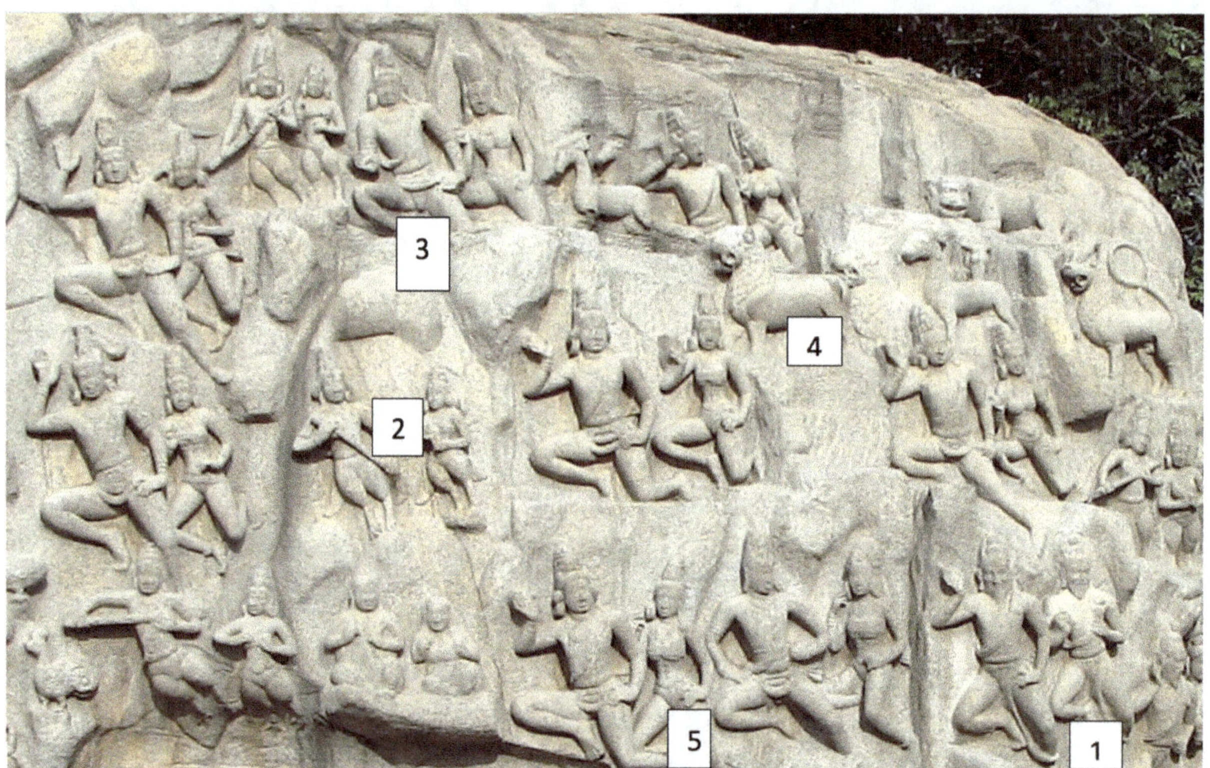

Fig.15: Depiction of Bhuvar Loka / Antariksha and the Flying semi divines

The categories of semi-divines are as follows:

Sadhyas - (Sages, marked No.1 in Fig. 15). They are depicted as peaceful old people with flowing beards, jatamakuta on their heads, and Yajnopavita. Sadhyas are a particular class of celestial beings and the accomplished deity of mantras.

Kinnaras - (Marked No.2), are a type of benevolent beings, deformed semi-divine mythical beings with a human form in the upper body and head. The lower body is with a bird's legs, wings, and feathers. Many Kinnaras are depicted with Kinnaris in a flying posture in the HR panel. In Hindu mythology, Kinnaras are known for their loyalty and service to gods and goddesses. Kinnaras are attendants of Kubera and Sarasvati, associated with Hindu gods for wealth and music, respectively. They entertain Gods with music. Since Kinnara also means a lute in Sanskrit, Kinnara is depicted with a lute or a vina in rock art. They are often mentioned in mythological narratives and considered messengers and good fortune carriers. They are also associated with natural environments, such as forests and mountains. Kinnaras may also be presented as half human and horse head in gentle forms and known for their musical skills. They are known for their romantic and harmonious relationships with their counterparts, Kinnaris (female Kinnaras).

Vidyadharas - (Marked No.3), are a group of supernatural beings, meaning the 'holders of Vidya' in Hinduism. They are semi-gods and attend to Lord Shiva. They are spirits of the air and are believed to fly. The Agni Puranas describe them as flying in the sky, either wearing or holding garlands and with karna kundalas(ring-like ear ornament).

Magical powers of Vidyadharas - (Marked No.4). Vidyadharas have magical powers and can decrease their size or show in other forms. They live in the Himalayas like other semi-divine beings like Kinnaras. The relief shows Vidyadhars in both personified and changed forms, as seen in numbers 3 and 4. Some animals, like a horse, lion, and deer, align with the flying gods of mid-zone in the HR panel, which may indicate the capacity of Vidyadhara's changed forms.

Flying Gandharvas and apsara couple - (Marked No.5). Vidyadharas and Gandharvas in sculptural representations share similarities but for a difference in ear ornaments. The Gandharva couple is associated with Hindu mythology as nature spirits and decorative elements. Gandharvas are celestial musicians and nature spirits known for their musical abilities and are associated with artistic and creative endeavors. Gandharva couples are portrayed in flying or dancing postures supporting their higher abode of atmosphere. They have youthful bodies and idealized graceful features, often adorned with celestial ornaments and jewelry. The male figure is depicted with a raised right-hand singing, and the female figure may be shown dancing or holding flowers. They are often depicted as participants in celestial events and are associated with the divine celestial Apsaras as their romantic partners.

Pitru figures:

The HR panel (in Fig. 16) depicts an old human couple in a sitting posture, playing cymbals and hence understood to be singing, eulogizing, or invoking the deity. Since they are in line with the flying Gandharva couple, it could represent Pitris (the forefathers of Bhagiratha), who are believed to abode in the zone above the earth in the pitruloka. Pitris are seated on Bhadrapitha (wooden seat). Since their body is smeared with ashes (Bhasma). They look a bit hazy and not sharp like other figures. There are over 5-6 such representations, all looking similar. They are waiting to see Ganga because she is the one who liberates them from debts (GS. 20, *Rinatraya vimochini*).

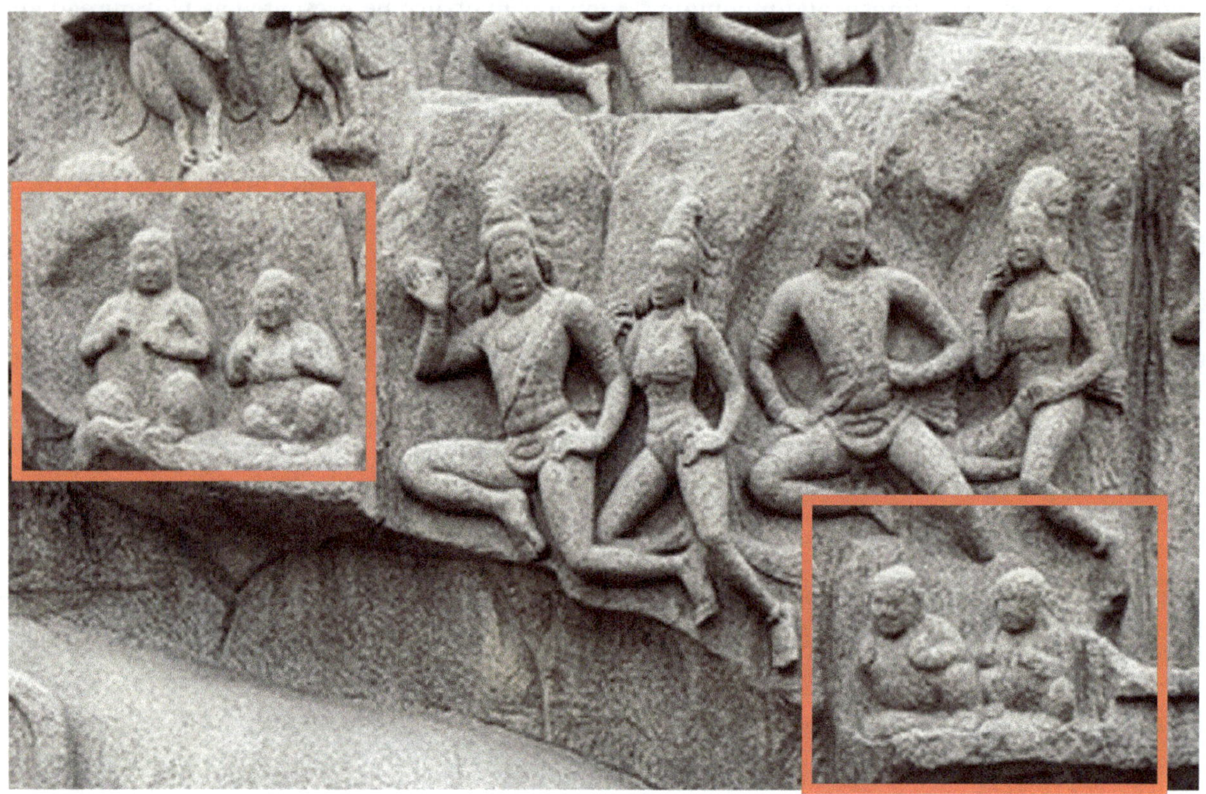

Fig.16: Depiction of Pitrus above the earthly level

2.I: Earth zone: Bhu Loka of mortals

In the HR panel, the sage Kapila is depicted reciting the chants before a temple nitch. Three figures without heads are sitting like ascetics in front of Kapila. The presence of three headless sadhus in front of Sage Kapila in the Bhagiratha episode holds symbolic significance. The story is: Bhagirata's great-grandfather, King Sagara of Suryavamsha, had conducted the Ashvamedha yaga. The Yaga horse was stolen by a demon who was also named Kapila and hid near sage Kapila's ashram. While searching for Aswamedha horse, King Sagara's three sons find it near sage Kapila's Ashram. They wrongly assume it to be sage Kapila's theft, and without paying any respect, they abuse the sage, humiliating him. The curse was inflicted on King Sagara's three sons, which resulted in their headless state and trapped due to their arrogance. The three headless sadhus in sitting posture in front of the nitch represent the three sons of King Sagara, Bhagiratha's ancestors waiting to be liberated from the curse by the flow of Ganga. Ganga is hence called *Sagaratmaja tarikai* (GS.7), one who liberated King Sagara's cursed sons.

The karmic consequences of the sons' disrespectful behavior towards Sage Kapila serve as a reminder of the importance of showing reverence and humility towards sages and enlightened beings.

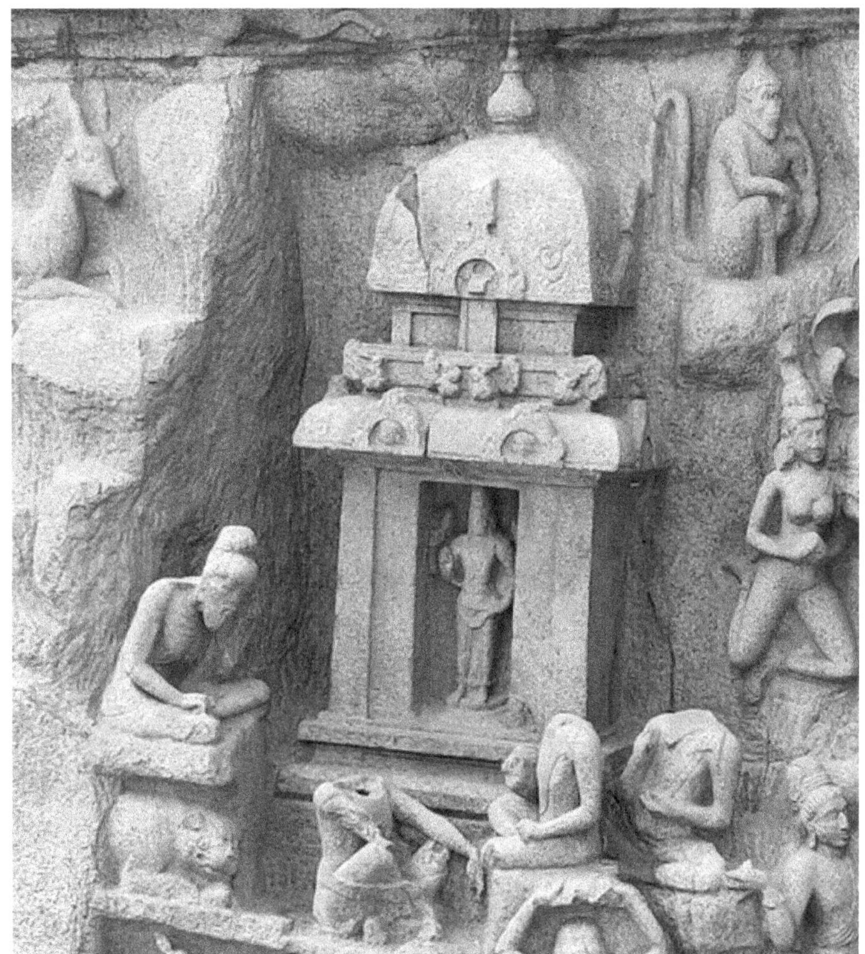

Fig. 17: Depiction of sage Kapila and the three cursed sons of king Sagara

Depiction of animals:

The posture and expression of curiosity in animals are well-defined. Both the wild and sober animals are together, forgetting their enmity. The scooping of rock material around each figure is not precise in the LR panel, and a larger area of depression is visible around the figures. This defect is not seen in the HR panel.

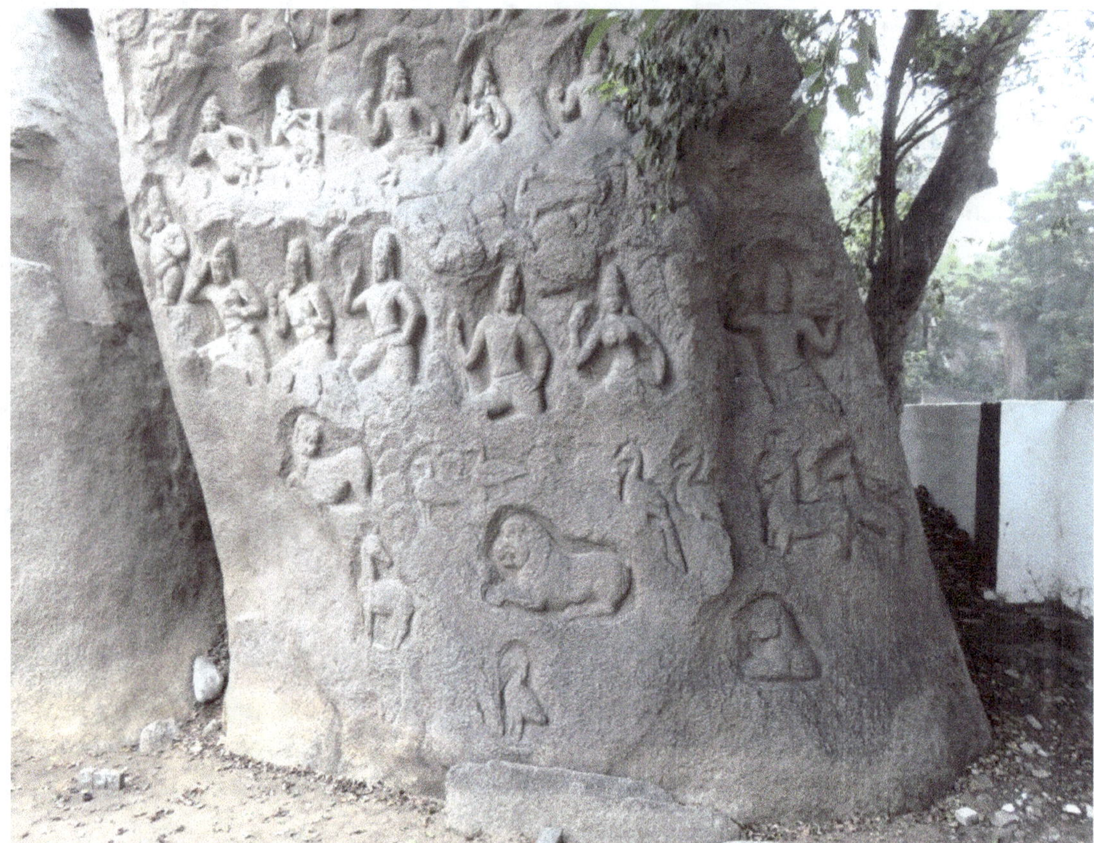

Fig.18: Depiction of animals in the LR panel

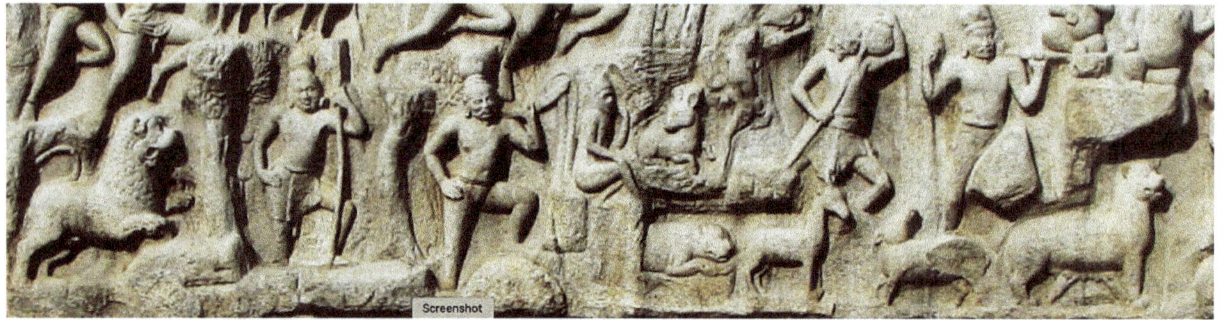

Fig 19. Depiction of Bhuloka, the animals and humans coexisting in the HR Panel

In the earth zone depiction in the LR panel, Fig.18, the animals like deer and birds are designed around the sitting lion, and much space on the rock surface is wasted.

In the HR panel Fig.19, The earth zone is defined at the bottom by depicting animals and ordinary people like woodcutters, and hunters, Rishi, all carrying objects used by them. The focus of all figures is towards the cleft where the waterfall was expected because Ganga is Duhkha *hantri* and *Daridra hantri* – who drives away sorrows and poverty (GS. 72 and 74). She is *Jagan Matri* (GS.101), the mother of the world. Ganga is called *Sapharipurnayai* GS.58) as the river was full of *Sapari* - meaning a glittering flying fish in Sanskrit, and the water was also a source for irrigation. In Fig 19, a man (the last figure) appears to be carrying various objects used by them and has a huge sac hung to a pole on his shoulder.

Along with them are animals like wild ones, herbivores, birds, amphibians, a monitor lizard, etc., all are aligned in a line as though they are rushing to watch the flow of Ganga. Ganga is called *Jangama*, the one who is moving, and *Jangamaadhara* (GS. 94 and 95) means one who is the sustainer of all living and moving. Jangama means on the move. Ganga is *Saranya*, meaning one who protects (GS.54) *and Jagad bhutayai* (GS.98), meaning benefactor and friend of what lives. There is a depiction of trees as Ganga is revered as *Jambudvipa viharini* (GS.102), meaning one who delights in the land of the rose apple tree. Amidst the human figures is the picture of a saint with a deer in front of him. Ganga is called *Shanti santana karini*(GS.73), meaning one who brings peace.

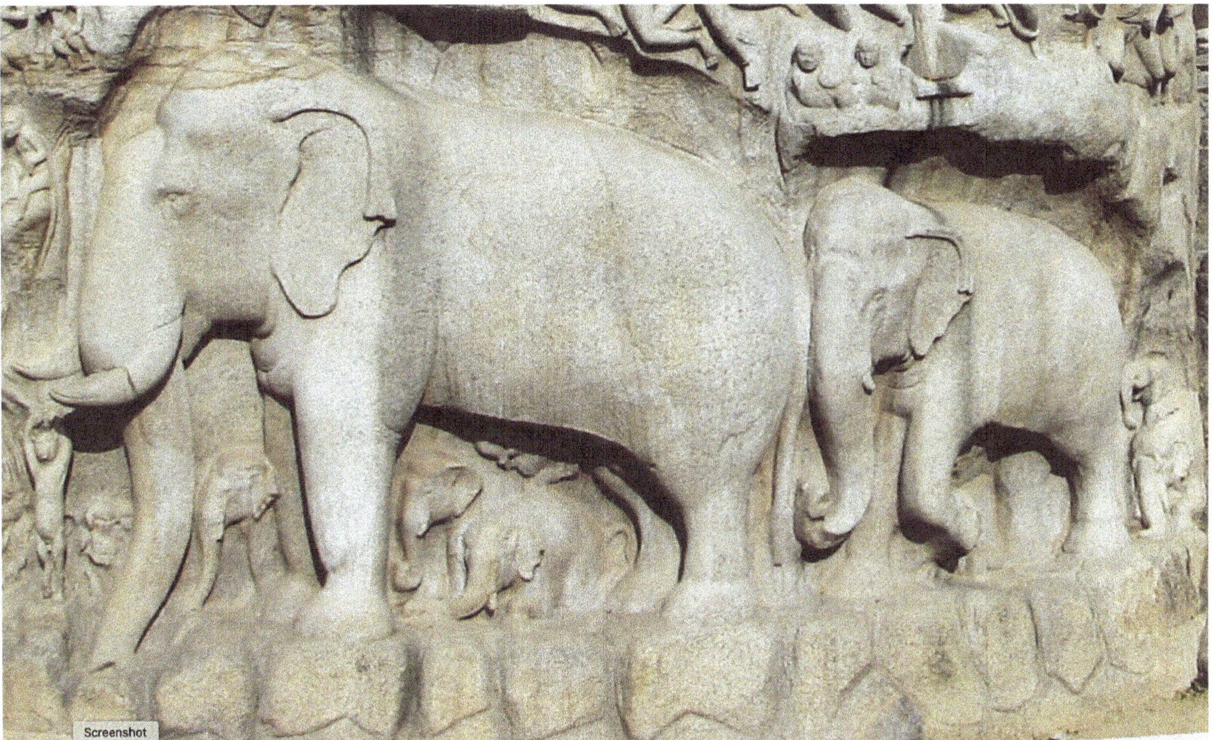

Fig 20. The herd of elephants in the HR panel

On the left side of the boulder, a family of elephants (Fig. 20) with several calves approaches the river to drink water. Elephants were essential in Pallava panels because they were central to the defense forces. All kings had elephants in great numbers. The bottom right part of the HR panel is unfinished. The dimension of this empty space in line with the opposite side was probably allocated to carve either the episode of sage Jahnu or another row of animals inhabiting the forests.

Adi Shankaracharya in Gangashtaka says *"Kari kalabha karakrantaram hastarangam"* meaning the water was full of waves created by the playful elephants and the calves beating the water by their trunks.

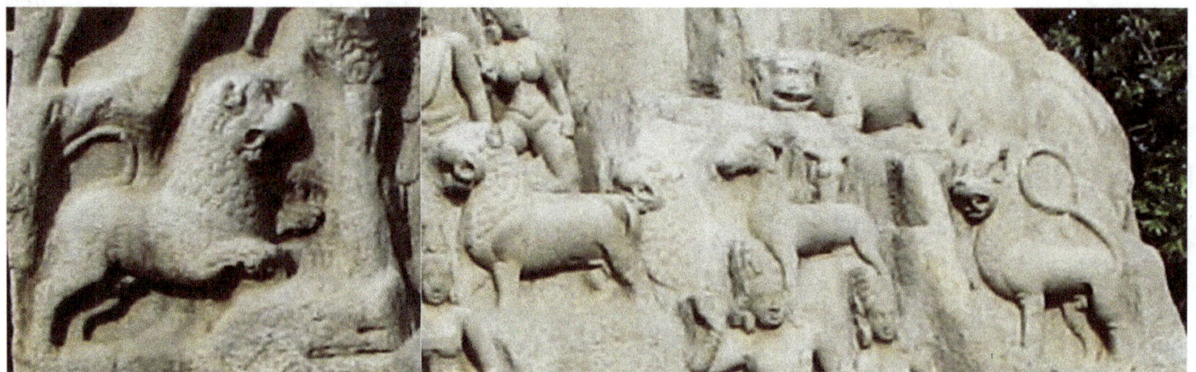

Fig.21. Depiction of lions in HR panels

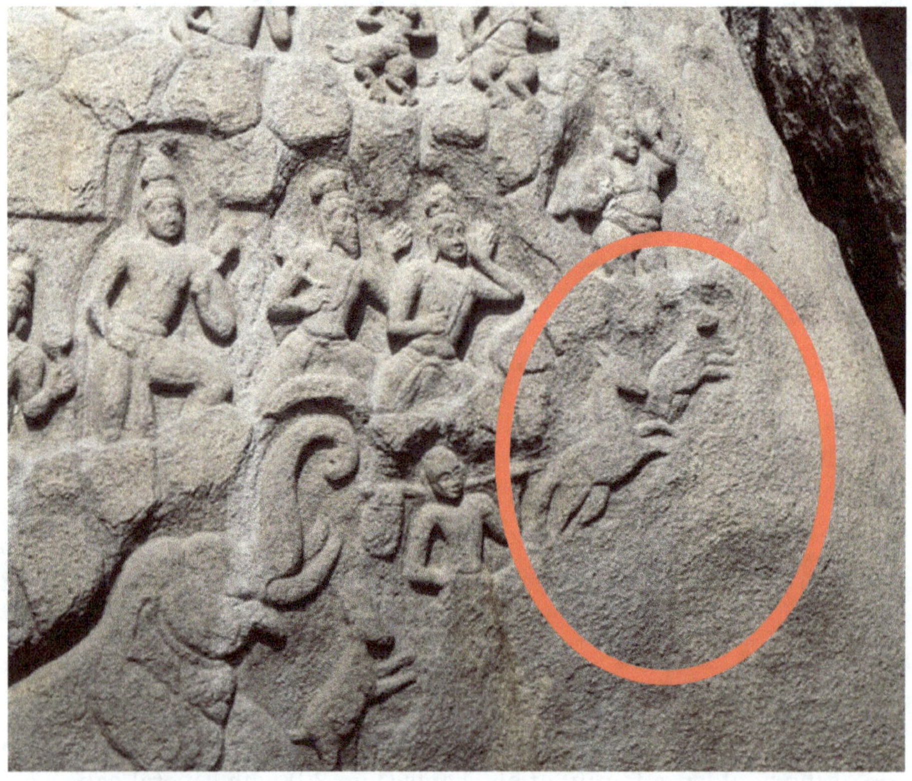

Fig. 22: Depiction of goats eagerly waiting to see the waterfall

The animal symbol associated with the Pallavas was the lion (Fig. 21). The lion was a prominent motif in Pallava art and architecture, particularly in rock-cut temples and stone sculptures. It was often depicted in various poses and forms, symbolizing power, strength, and royalty. The lion symbol was significant in conveying the grandeur and authority of the Pallava dynasty and reflecting their cultural and religious beliefs. The lion motifs in great numbers can be seen here. They are also on the pillars, temple entrances, and sculptures in the Pallava architectural marvels, such as the rock relief carvings, Shore Temple in Mamallapuram, and the Kailasanatha Temple in Kanchipuram.

The LR panel (Fig. 22) shows the mountain goats on rocks (Marked in red circle) eagerly waiting to see the event of water falling from the sky. The posture and depiction of curiosity are worth noticing.

2.J: The underground: Patala Loka

Half-human-half snake figures slither up a crevice in the HR panel.

The Naga devas (Serpent deities) with the human body and hoods attached to the back are at the bottom of the cleft and rise up from the underground Patala loka (Fig. 23).

Their categories of 7, 5, and 3-headed Nagas (Nagarajas) are depicted with their consort Nagins. The snakes inhabiting the underworld are rising, some holding Anjali hasta, and some are with an object in hand, welcoming Ganga and paying their reverence. The serpent deities are not depicted in the LR panel.

Marjala Sanyasi: Representation of fake ascetics

The cat and mice figures on the rock surface are exciting and are like a simile.

Near the snake-headed figures, the HR panel represents a cat in a standing posture, like penance, with one leg raised. Many mice are depicted around it (Fig. 24). It is a simile to "*Marjala sanyasa*" where a cat pretends initially to be a non-harming saint and tries to win the confidence of the mice group. Later, he begins to consume rats one after the other as the mice foolishly trust the cat.

The intention of this could be that even the fake sanyasis are part of society, and they, too, have shown curiosity to witness the descent of Ganga. The concept of a fake person is an abstract thought conveyed through a figure in a simile. The fake sanyasis are also hinted to belong to the lower zone of social order.

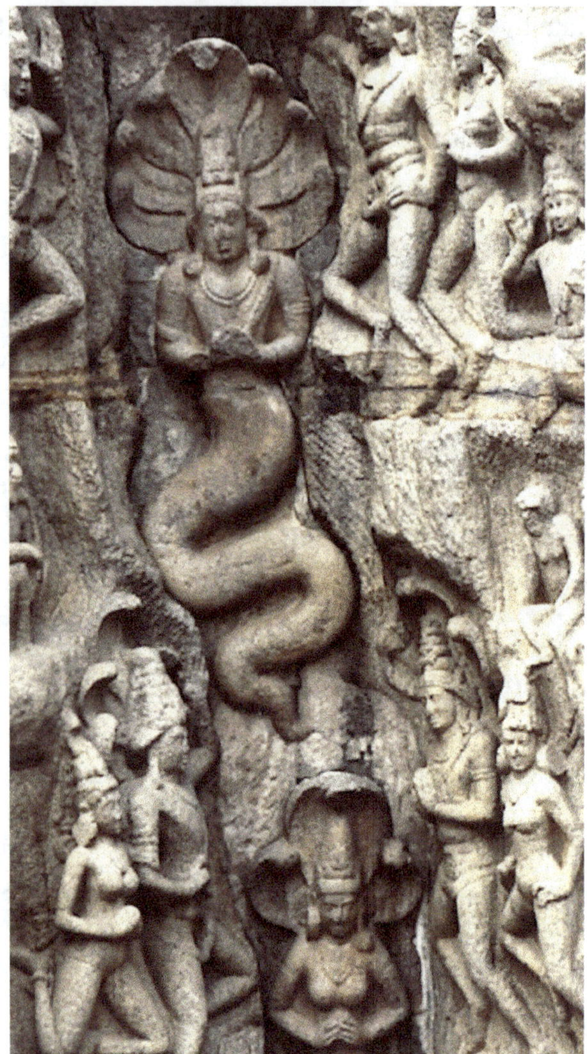

Fig.23: The serpent deities Nagas paying reverence

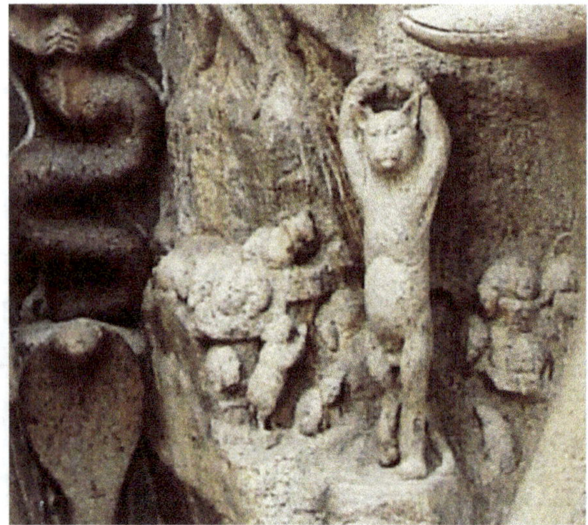

Fig 24. Depiction of the fake person as Marjala Sanyasi

Depiction of pious men waiting to receive Ganga

The picture in the HR panel Fig. 25, depicts four men in similar dress codes near the water at a flowing level. One of them carries a pot on his left shoulder to collect the sacred waters of Ganga and carries a ritual offering in his right hand (Could be a lamp) to wave the light to the river Ganga on her descent. The man beside him also holds a ritual object in his left hand, looking down at the water. These two men are in a headdress of jatamakuta where locks of hair are tied into a bun above the head. It is usually given to ascetics.

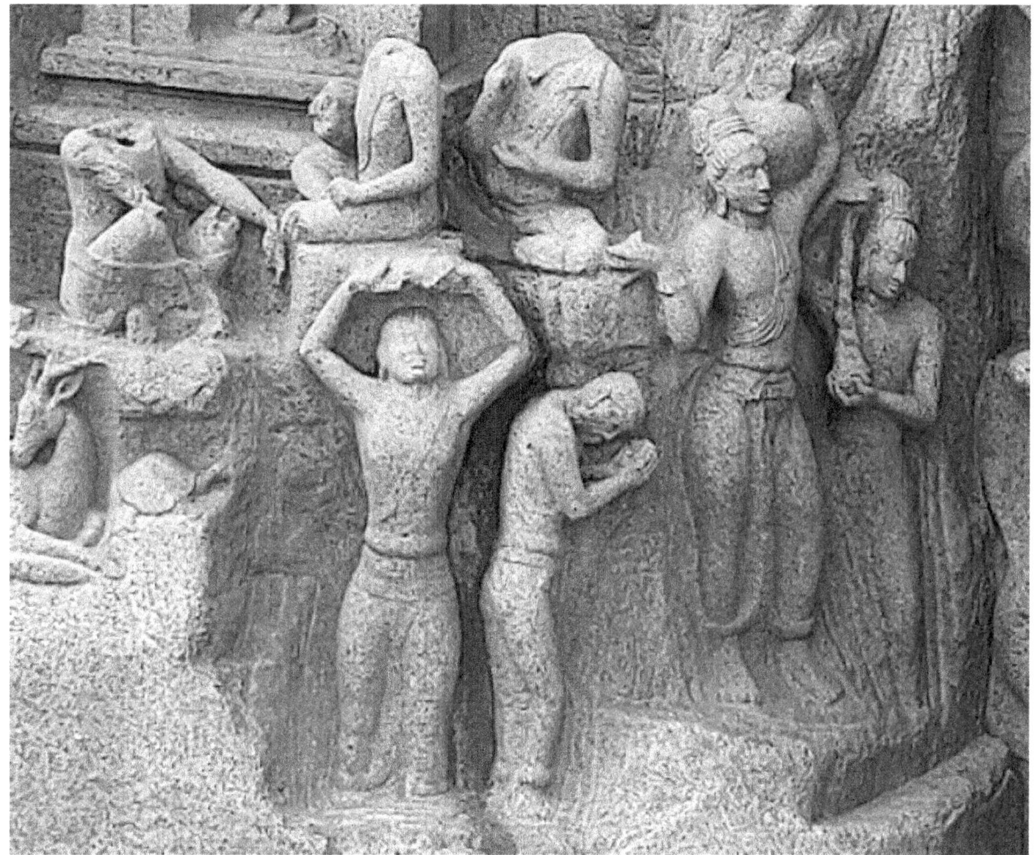

Fig 25: Depiction of pious men waiting to wave a lamp to Ganga

Rigveda Mandala 10.30 says *"Go to the reservoir O Adhvaryus, worship the waters, child with your oblations."*

The two men are the Adhvaryu priests (Yajurveda priests who perform the manual part of a ritual).

Adi Shankaracharya in Gangashtaka says *"Sayam prathar muneenaam kusa kusuma chayai"*, meaning saints were giving the dawn and dusk salutations with water that was full of floating grass and flowers.

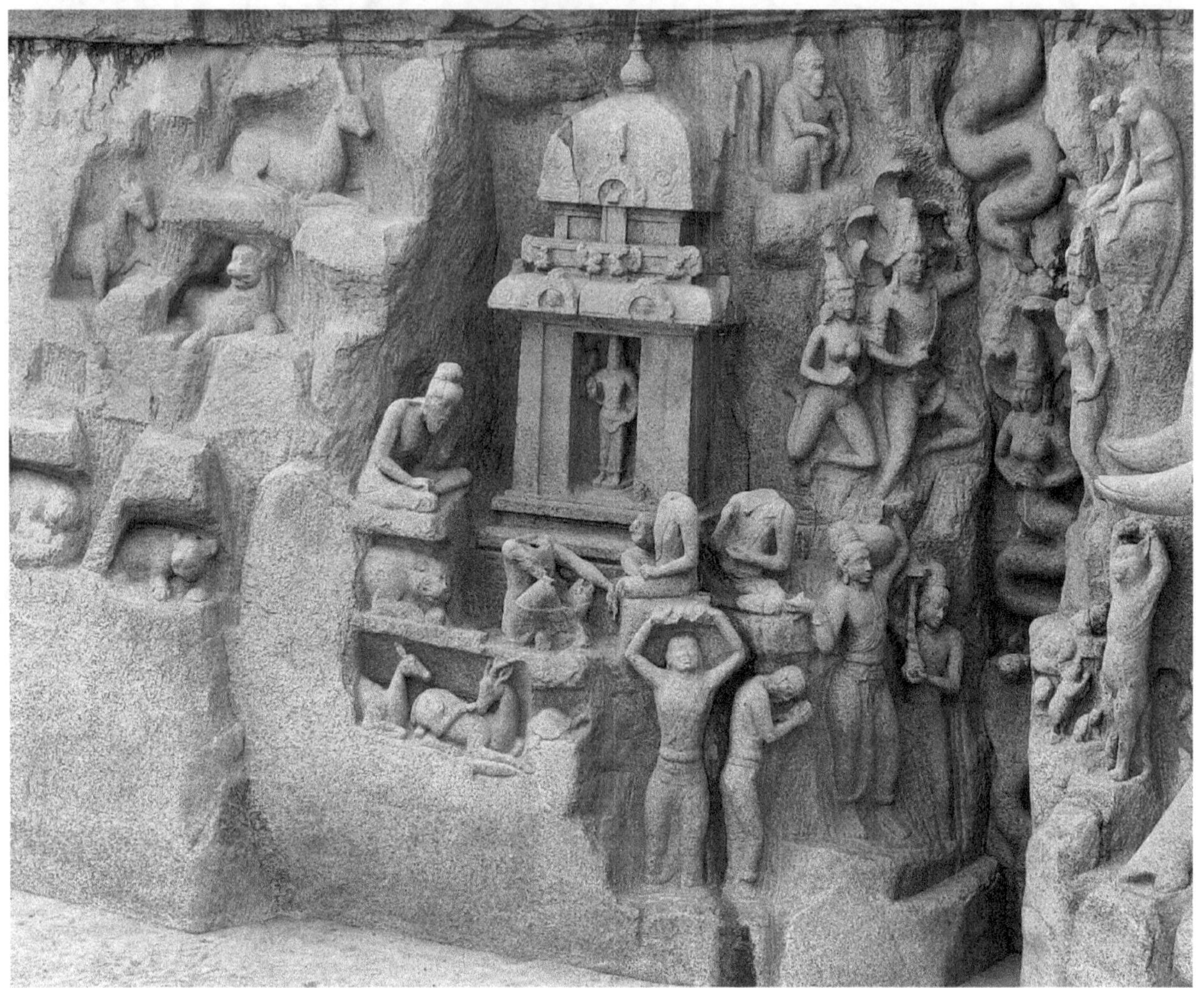

Fig 26. Depiction of pious men waiting to receive Ganga

The two men are descending the steps to reach the water flow level. Ganga is called *Swarga sopana Sarani* (GS.69) meaning river Ganga is like a ladder to heaven. The steps are an indication of Sopana meaning steps. (Fig. 26). Two steps are indicated where men are standing for them to get down to the water and fetch water in their pots because Ganga is Virinchi *kalasha vasai* (GS.45) one who is residing in the water pot. The water is *Amritakara salila,* meaning the water that is as good as nectar (GS.43) . Ganga water is called *Nitya suddha* (GS.28) meaning pure because in upper Himalayan stretches, the number of bacteriophages is much more. Hence scientifically, it is confirmed that the purity of the Ganga is due to bacteriophages, which do not allow bacterial growth and since the oxygen content is higher than any other river in the world, it remains fresh for more extended periods.

These men with a pot on their shoulder, at the base of the rock relief is a significant sculpture with historical and cultural significance. It is interpreted as an illustration of a severe drought that

40

plagued the region, causing a severe water shortage. In response, the sage Bhagiratha performed intense penance and received a boon from Lord Shiva, allowing the divine river Ganga to descend to Earth, not only liberating the trapped souls of his forefathers in the ash mound but also providing water for the people. Standing firmly on the ground with his hands lifted up, one man looks at the sky for waterfalls, and the other is holding Namaskara mudra, a gesture of salutation, respect, and devotion. Ganga is *Satya sandha Priya* (GS.61) meaning beloved of faithful devotees. The hand gesture is commonly used in Hindu rituals and ceremonies. The depiction proves the power of divine intervention in the face of adversity.

2.K: Another Gangadhara Shiva panel in the Pallava style

Kailasanathar temple at Kancheepuram of Pallava architecture was built in 7th Cen.CE by the Pallava king Narasimhavarman II. Most of the Pallava rulers were Brahmanical Hindus and worshippers of Shiva. The town of Kanchipuram was the capital of the imperial Pallavas. NarasimhaVarman was also known as Rajasimha, had a peaceful reign. His period is chiefly known for his remarkable architectural activities in the Dravidian temple style. Of the many temples he built, the most famous one is Kailasanathar or the Rajasimheshvara temple of Kanchi.

The capital of the Pallava dynasty was named Kanchipuram, also spelled as Kanchi. The name "Kanchipuram" has historical significance and is believed to have been derived from multiple sources. According to a local legend, Kanchipuram was once a city of immense prosperity and grandeur, and deities were adorned with ornaments made of gold, and hence it was called "Kancheepuram" or the "Golden City." Kanchi also means the decorative girdle belt. Kanchi in Sanskrit means a curve. The city is located in a region where the river Kaveri takes a curved course. Kanchi may also be a metaphoric expression of the curved course of the river. The origin of the name "Kanchipuram" may not be definitively known, but the city remains an essential part of India's cultural and historical heritage.

The Kailasanathar temple pillars are adorned with lion (Simha)figures at the base.

There are two parts to the temple. The inner face of the complex wall is fitted with small shrines known as devakulikas in which many panels of Lord Shiva are seen. Gangadhara Shiva with Parvati is one of the Shiva panels. Though the figure is sandstone, the temple's foundation is granite.

Gangadhara Shiva Panels:

The two panels of Gangadhara Shiva are almost similar and look like two different sculptors made them, as the facial expression of Shiva looks different.

The two panels are analyzed in this book as Panel 1 and Panel 2.

Panel 1 has a beautiful figure of Shiva as Gangadhara with Parvati. On both sides of the frame are two huge lion figures. The lion was the animal symbol associated with the Pallavas as a prominent motif in all the Pallava art and architecture and also at the base of all pillars. The canine teeth and the back legs' claws draw viewers' attention. The lion symbol probably signified the Pallava royalty's power, strength, and grandeur. The name of the early Pallava king was Simha varman. (Simha means a lion) and his name was probably immortalized with a lion motif by the following rulers.

At the base is the figure of an elephant revered in religion and respected for its prowess in war. Although the lion was their insignia that served as a base to their pillars, it is the elephant they appeared to have been most fond of as they occupy many other niches of their architecture. The creativity of the Pallavas did not diminish throughout their reign despite being constantly at war with the Chalukyas from the north.

Shiva shows the stylized Pallava way of making the headdress an extra-long crown. The Jatamakuta is almost twice the height of the face (One tala) as seen in the panel. The headdress is with shiromala, a thick round fillet or diadem like a halo at the back. Shiva is four-armed. Shiva has stretched a string of matted hair in his left hand and supports it with the middle finger. The hand gesture is vismaya mudra. The other backhand is positioned in Kapittha gesture, showing where he would have held the other string of his matted hair. His front right hand is on his pelvic part in Katyavalambita's hand gesture (of being ready to help). He wears a short costume, and his legs are in the heroic Alidha posture.

Parvati, to the left of Shiva, is in a graceful posture but depicted as scared of the fall of Ganga and trying to run away. She wears a long costume adorned with anklets, bangles, and a tall crown.

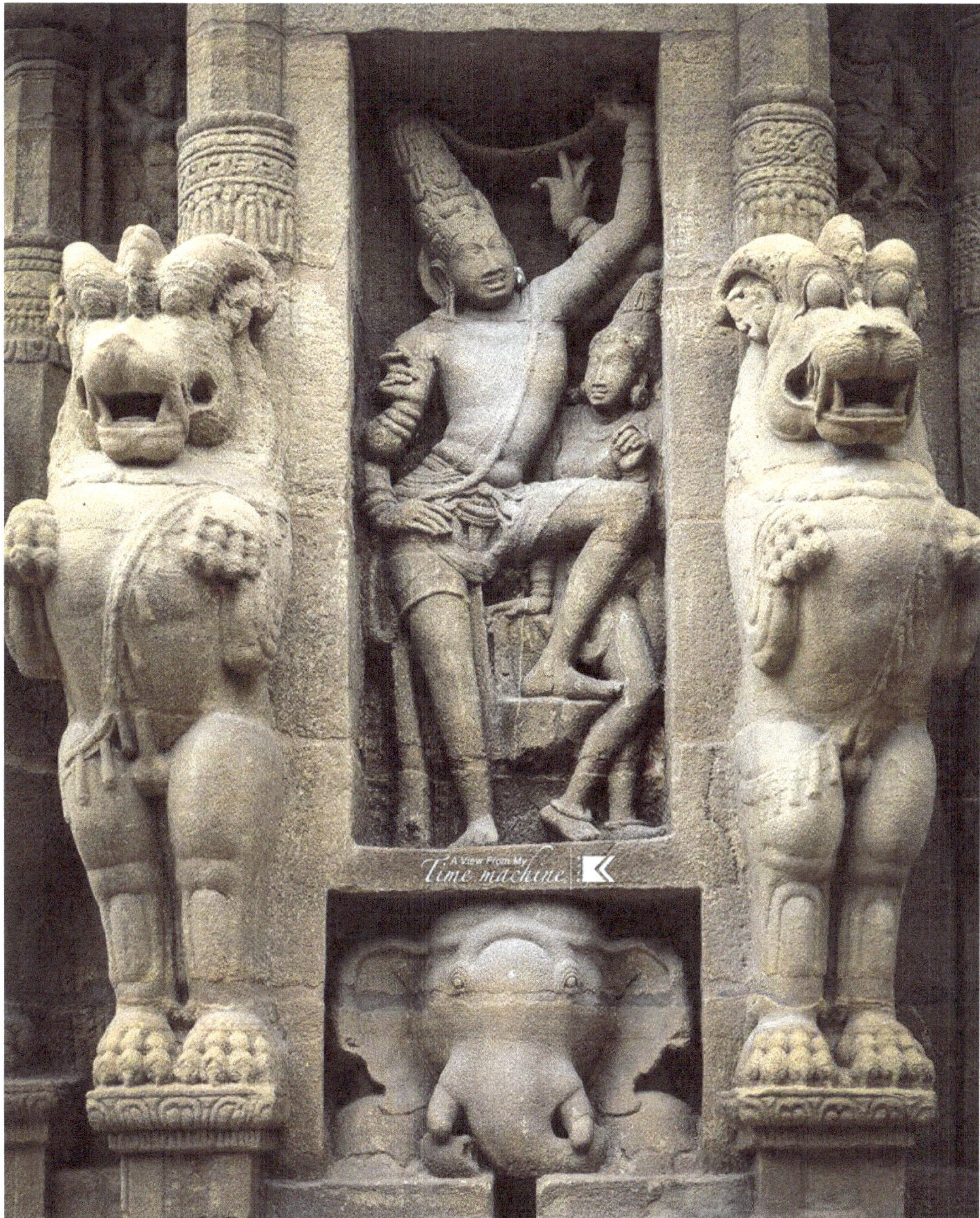

Fig. 27. Gangadhara Shiva, Panel 1, from Kailasanathar temple at Kancheepuram

According to the Puranic story, Once, while sage Narada was describing the beauty and purity of river Ganga, Parvati / Uma expressed her desire to see the sacred river Ganga. Narada warns Uma about the powerful current of Ganga. Shiva tries to satisfy Uma's desire to witness Ganga and also care for her safety. He locks the force of Ganga in his hair locks and lets a small stream of the river through his jata. Uma was mesmerized by the beauty and purity of Ganga the celestial water flowing from heaven or descending from heaven and blessing the Earth with her grace. Parvati accepts Ganga as her sister. Ganga is described in Ganga stotra as *Uma sahodarye* (GS.107) meaning sister of Uma / Parvati.

The two figures are beautifully carved to show the eternal masculine energy and form of Shiva and the eternal feminine grace and energy of Parvati.

The panel does not show Ganga (probably for lack of space and Shiva is in the *Ganga Jatadhara* pose. The symbol of "Sengol" is tucked in Shiva's garment.

In Panel 2. of Fig. 28, Shiva is depicted in a ferocious form with a muscular body. He stamps his left foot on the shoulder of a demon. Shiva's jatamakuta is high and looks more than two times the length of the face. His stretch of a jata is held in the left arm and with another left hand, he is squeezing the hair to release a small stream of water.

Parvati /Uma looks very graceful, wearing a decorative kirita makuta.

She looks scared in her posture of quick-paced steps. Her face shows an amazed expression, and her eyes look at the water's fall. She holds Shiva's knee part in fear. She

Ganga -Though she is depicted in a personified form, the river's flow looks like a huge wave. Ganga wears a crown, and hands are folded in Anjali mudra. She is shown cascading down from his hair, symbolizing the divine and life-giving nature of the river.

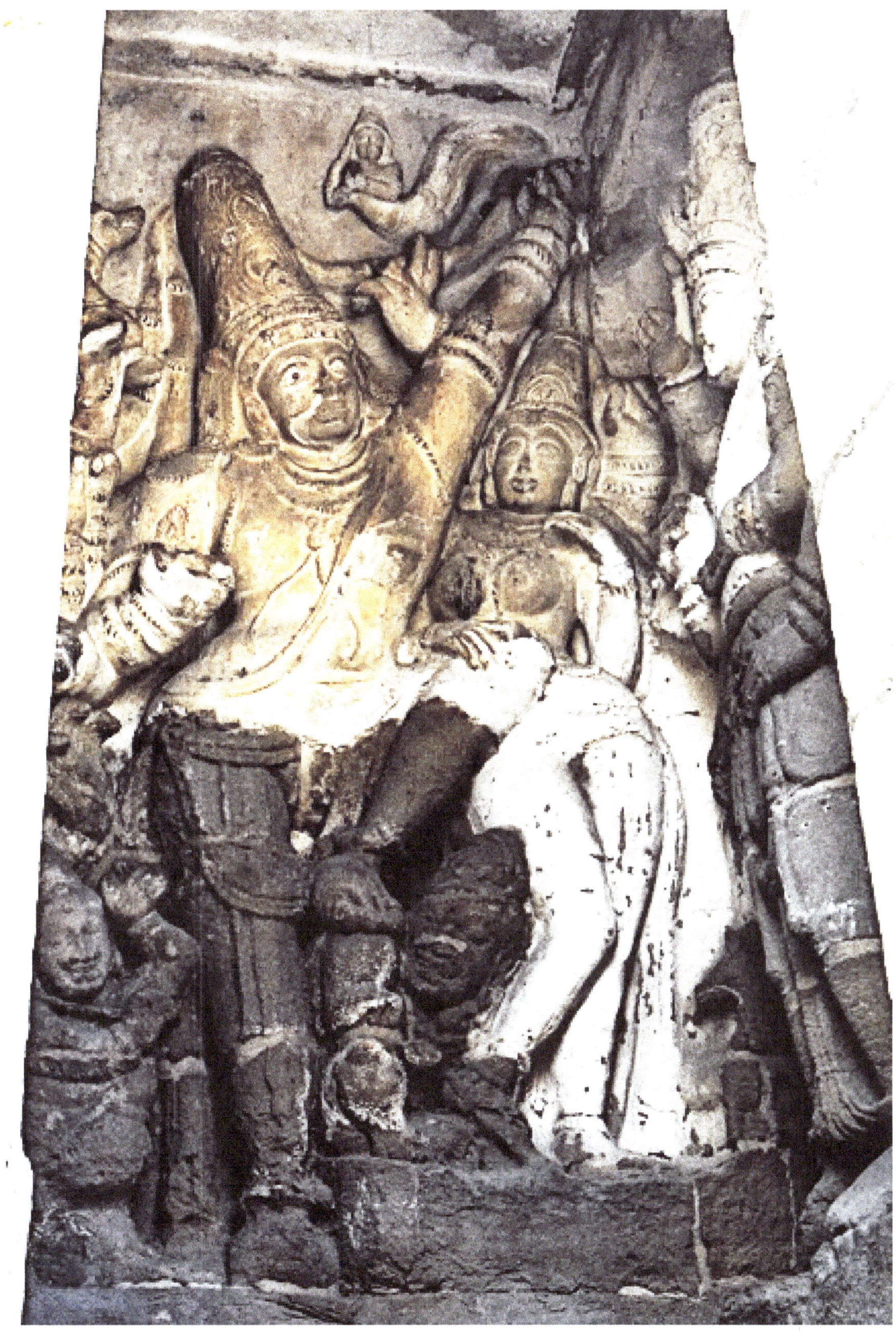

Fig. 28. Gangadhara Shiva, Panel 2, from Kailasanathar temple at Kancheepuram

3.   Gangavatarana in the Early Chalukyan Style at Aihole

The episode of Bhagirataprayatna highlighting the figure of Bhagirata is depicted in many temples in India.

Fig. 29 is the Bhagirata prayatna panel from RavanaPhadi cave, Aihole, Karnataka. It belongs to the Early Chalukyas of the 6th Cen. CE. The Chalukyas of Badami, also known as the Early Chalukyas or the Chalukyas of Vatapi, were a powerful dynasty that ruled a significant part of the Deccan region from the 6th to the 8th century CE. Pulakeshin I founded the dynasty in the 6th century CE, and their power reached its zenith under Pulikeshin II in the early 7th Cen CE when he subjugated the rebellious feudatories of neighboring states. But later, he was killed by the Pallava rulers. Chalukyas, though were orthodox worshippers of Hindu Gods, supported other faiths of Jainism and Buddhism.

The subsequent rulers of the Chalukya dynasty continued to support and propagate Shaivism, which venerates Lord Shiva as the supreme deity. They constructed numerous temples dedicated to Lord Shiva, with Aihole, Pattadakal, and Badami being notable sites showcasing their architectural and religious patronage and hence upgraded as a UNESCO World Heritage site.

Aihole, located in present-day Karnataka, was one of their essential centers, known for its architectural wonders and temples. The Aihole monuments are in red Sandstone.

Ravanaphadi cave temple was built in 550.CE has many beautiful figures of Shiva of which the Bhagirata episode is one of the panels depicted like a tableau.

Stylistically, the slender figures have very masculine physiques adorned with pleated costumes, close lines, and heavy ornamentation. All male deities have a unique way of crossing the multiple pearled neck ornament over the right shoulder. The crowns are long and conical.

The picture shows an emaciated Bhagiratha in deep penance standing on one leg. Ganga with her two headstreams is together depicted as three goddesses in one arc-shaped flowery structure. Shiva has opened his matted hair in the back two hands to hold the force involved in river Ganga's descent. Parvati is standing to the left of Shiva in graceful form.

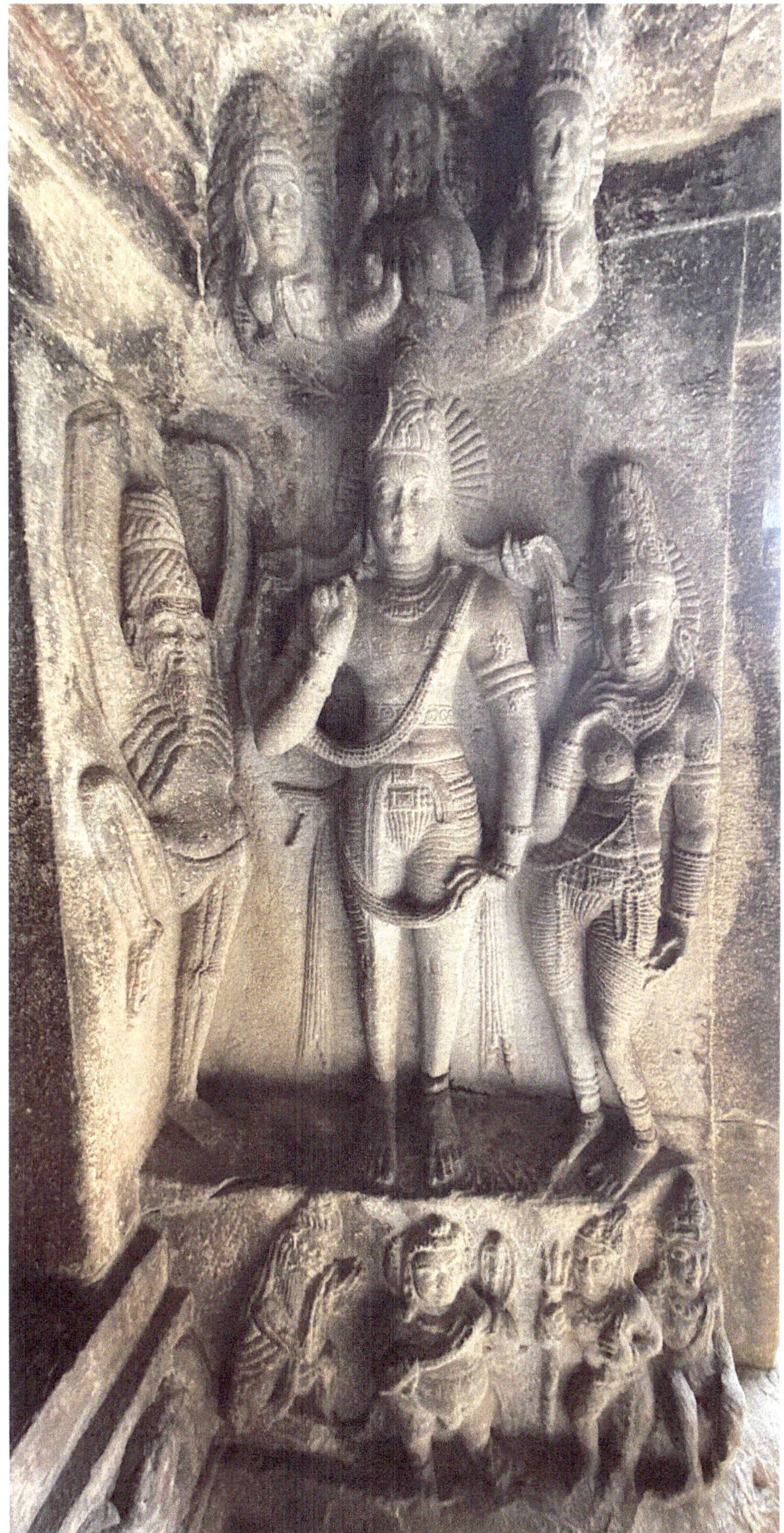

Fig. 29: Gangavatarana / Bhagirata Prayatna in the early Chalukyan style of Aihole

The story of the flow of the river Ganga from heaven to earth is one of the most popular episodes of Hindu mythology. According to the legend, King Bhagiratha belonged to the Ikshvakyu dynasty and was an ancestor of King Dasharatha and Sri Rama. Bhagirata's great grandfather, King Sagara of Suryavamsha, and his 60000sons had been turned to ashes by the sage Kapila's curse for disturbing him with noise and abuse at his abode. The heap of ashes remained without any purification rituals. The cursed sons of King Sagara could attain salvation only if they were washed in the holy waters of the Ganga. King Bhagiratha, after ascending Ayodhya's throne, determined to fulfill his ancestors' salvation, embarked on an intense, rigorous penance, praying to the creator of the universe, Lord Brahma, to release Ganga from heaven. Lord Brahma granted his wish but cautioned about the immense force involved during the descent of Ganga. Bhagiratha prayed to Lord Shiva who opened his matted locks, allowing the Ganga to flow through them, skillfully directing her flow and preventing catastrophic damage.

Shiva holds the locks of hair in the backhands on both sides in a hand gesture called "*Kapittha hasta*". One of the uses of this hand gesture according to Natyashastra is *"Vesthane"* meaning winding- to twist or curl. After spreading the matted locks of hair, Shiva has been squeezing it to let the water flow in a controlled way that was trapped in his hair. Water drops are also depicted from both sides. These are the symbolic representations of the mighty river Ganga flowing in channels as tributaries. The front right hand also holds Kapittha hand gesture in which he holds a small flower. Shiva stands in *Samabhanga* where both legs are firmly placed on the ground.

The left hand is placed on the upper thigh in *"Katyavalambita mudra"* which indicates a gesture of being ready to help. Shiva is not depicted here with the usual accessories like the trident, damaru, parashu, and mriga in his hands.

Regarding the adornments, Shivas' head shows the tuft of the lock of hair high as Jata Makuta adorned with the crescent moon. He is called *Tripurari-siras-cuda* (GS.21). He shows a halo (Prabhavali) indicative of divine status. The third eye is also well-defined. On the ears are the kundalas. Upper arms are decorated with snake bands called Keyura. The neck is adorned with a necklace and a garland of beads that is depicted over the right arm (A style of early Chaukya style). He wears a short costume and a cloth tied around the waist has the two edges are falling freely on both sides.

Parvati holds Vismaya mudra in her right hand near the chin, admiring the beauty of the river Ganga falling down and the heroic act of Shiva. She is adorned with a decorative high crown, with the halo, kundalas in ears, multi-layered pearl chain on the neck. Arms are adorned with bands called Angada in the upper arm and Kankana,a bracelet on the wrist below the elbows. The waist, below the navel, is decorated with pearly strings of waistband called Dabu. The feet are adorned with ornaments of small bells called kinkini and other anklets. She is in a short costume above knee level and stands in a graceful posture.

The three river goddesses above Shiva's head are also adorned with Karanda makuta with a halo (Prabhavali) , neck ornaments, and ear ornaments. Ganga and two more rivers, depicted only in the upper body are in a personified form holding Anjali mudra and with a halo indicative of the divine status. River Ganga is depicted in the Chalukyan art with the two turbulent headstreams Bhagirathi and Alakananda, all three in personified form of river goddesses with haloes and holding Anjali mudra. Ganga is hence called *Triveni* (GS.46) meaning the three divisions of a braid, and *Trigunatmakayai* (GS.47), one with the three gunas of Sattva, Rajas, and Tamas. Ganga, since she is called Omkara roopini(GS.66) the three rivers trace along with the jata can be seen tracing the "OM" symbol.

Adi Shankaracharya has quoted in Gangastakam that *"Bhooya shambhu jata vibhooshana mani jjahnor maharsheriyam,"* meaning Ganga became an ornamental gem on the head of Lord Shiva, and then later was born as the daughter of sage Jahnu. Ganga is depicted in the panel as adorning the head of lord Shiva.

Lord Shiva has opened his matted hair to resist the flow of Ganga's stream. Ganga is also called *Bhagitati* (GS.11) and *Bhagirata rathanugayai (GS.13)* – meaning one who followed the ratha (of devotion) of Bhagirata.

Bhagirata has an emaciated body and wears a kaupina loin cloth. Hair is twisted and tied into long cap like Jatamakuta. The peaceful face shows that he is engrossed in penance. Bhagiratha has an uplifting position of hands holding chin mudra or Jnanamudra.. He shows three lined marks on his forehead and has a long beard and mustaches. The left leg is firm on the ground, and the right leg is raised up to the "Urdhvajanu" position, in which the right knee is held up to the level of breasts. The foot is in kunchita foot pointing downwards. During her flow, Ganga reached the ashes of King Sagara's sons and washed over them, granting salvation.

Ayudha purushas of Shiva

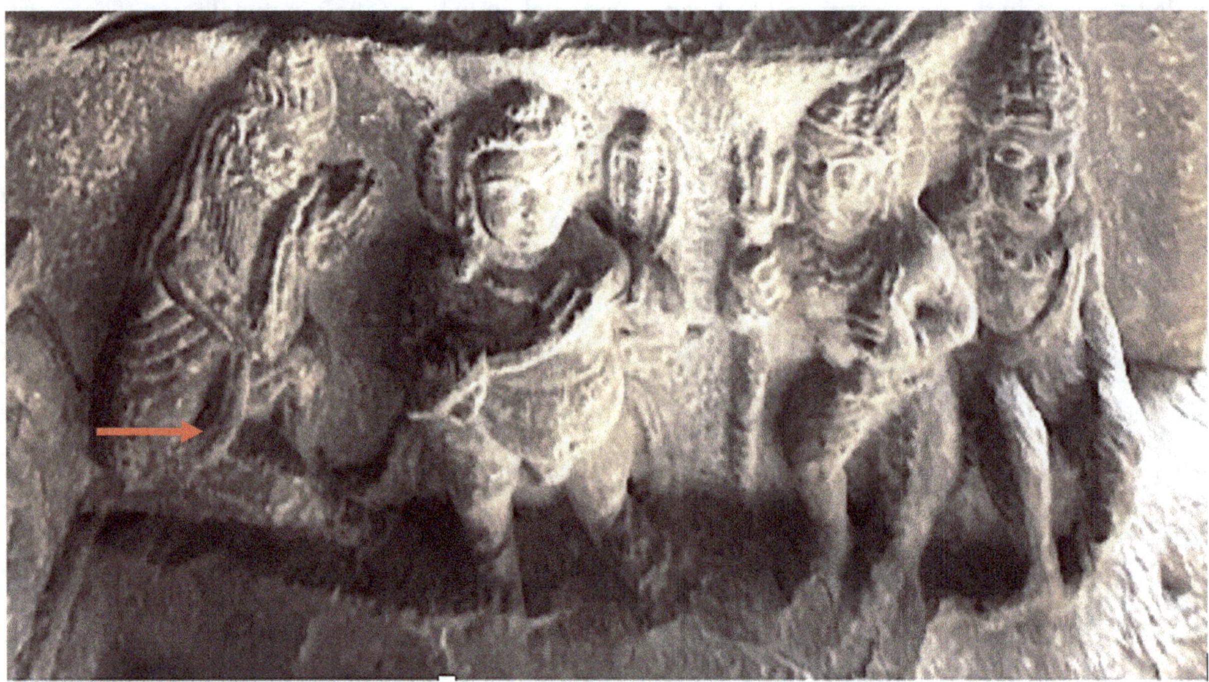

Fig. 30: Ayudha Purushas are associated with Shiva and Sage Jahnu

The panel below the figures of Shiva and Parvati are four figures (Fig 30).They are some of the prominent Ayudha Purushas associated with Lord Shiva. They embody different aspects of his power, symbolism, and cosmic role.

The torrential flow of Ganga through the Jata of Shiva was still forceful, and she flowed, destroying the farm and Penance of sage Jahnu. Jahnu gets so angry at the damage caused that he consumes the Ganga water in one gulp to teach her a lesson. The figure of the old sage in the picture shows sage Jahnu holding the entire water of Ganga in his hands, gulping it. But the devas and Bhagirata pray to him, telling him about the unliberated status of Bhagirata's fore fathers, and requesting him release Ganga. Sage Jahnu then releases Ganga through his ear, and Ganga thus becomes Jahnhavi, the daughter of Sage Jahnu. The flow of Ganga (marked with a red arrow) as a thin stream can be seen coming out of the sage's right ear.

In Hindu mythology and iconographic representations, Ayudha Purushas are the divine entities associated with the weapons or objects wielded by a deity. They are often considered personifications or manifestations of the powers and attributes of the respective deity. Since the main figure of Shiva is without his iconographic accessories, they are represented like Ayudha purushas in a personified form. The base part of the panel depicts four figures. The first one is Sage Jahnu, depicted as a yogi in emaciated form.

Here are some prominent Ayudha Purushas of Shiva:

- **Vasuki:** The personification of the serpent Vasuki wound around Shiva's neck is an ayudha purusha here. Vasuki is in a personified form like Shiva and a cobra hood by the side of the neck is depicted in a running posture. The left hand shows Danda hasta,the arm thrown forward and held straight across the chest, imitating the flow of the serpent.

- **Trishula**: The trident,of Shiva is known as Trishula, which is one of the primary weapons of Lord Shiva. It symbolizes the destruction of ignorance and ego. The three prongs also symbolize the three aspects of time—past, present, and future. Trishula is in a personified ayudha purusha form like the deity holding the trident in the right hand and a standing posture.

- **Damaru:** The last figure seated shows a prominent third eye, holding Damaru. Damaru is a small two-headed drum associated with Lord Shiva. It represents the cosmic sound AUM, which is the primordial sound of creation. Damaru symbolizes rhythm, resonance, and the cyclic nature of existence.

The panel depicting the entire episode of Ganga's descent is carved beautifully in the red sandstone. The stylized features of the early Chalukya art look at its best in the Ravanphadi cave panel of Gangadhara Shiva. The depiction of Ayudha purushas associated with Shiva is a unique representation here.

4. Gangavatarana in the Rashtrakuta Style at Elephanta and Ellora Caves

Rashtrakuta architecture flourished primarily between the 6th and 9th centuries CE in the Deccan region of India and is renowned for its impressive temple architecture and exquisite sculptures. The stabilization of Rashtrakuta dynasty began with Dantidurga. Krishna, I ascended the throne after him and defeated the power of Chalukyas and Gangas. Krishna I (reign 756–774 CE),took charge of the growing Rashtrakuta Empire, which got consolidated during his time. His son Dhruva began a new era in the history of Rashtrakutas.

The Rashtrakuta rulers built Elephanta caves and the Ellora rock-cut temple, both dedicated to Lord Shiva.   Elephanta caves are located 30 km away from the district in Aurangabad district of Maharashtra state in Western India located on the Elephanta Island (otherwise known as the Island of Gharapuri). It features two hillocks separated by a narrow valley. There are about 7 caves.

The magnificent rock-cut temples of Ellora are in northwest Maharashtra state, Western India. It is located near the village of Ellora, 30 km away from Aurangabad, and 80 km southwest of the Ajanta Caves.

The exact date of the construction of the Elephanta Caves is uncertain, but they are believed to have been built between the 5th and 8th centuries CE. Some scholars believe that the earlier caves at both Elephanta and Ellora to have been constructed during the reign of Krishnaraja of the Kalachuri dynasty, who ruled between 6-7th Cen CE in the regions of Gujarat, Maharashtra, and Madhya Pradesh. The date of Elephanta caves is a much-debated topic and varies from 6th to 8th Cen CE. The specific details about the builders and the exact construction timeline are not definitively known due to the lack of inscriptions or historical records at the site.

Kailasa Ellora rock cut temple was built in the eighth century by Rashtrakuta king Krishna I in 756-773 CE. A copper plate grant from Baroda of the period of Karka II (813 CE) speaks about the greatness of this edifice. This clarifies that the Kailasa Ellora temple was in 8th Cen CE.

Both Elephanta Caves and Kailasa Ellora are, designated as UNESCO World Heritage Site, for they have remarkable sculptures and intricate carvings that offer a glimpse into the rich cultural and religious history of India.

The Rashtrakuta temples, constructed from Basalt rocks, feature elaborate narrative panels depicting stories from Hindu mythology. These panels are often arranged sequentially, allowing visitors to follow the storyline while circumambulating the temple.

The Gangadhara figures at both places are adorned with narrative panels of celestial beings, such as Gandharvas, Apsaras, Kinnaras, and Vidhyadharas. These figures are shown in various poses and engaged in diverse activities, adding a celestial charm to the architecture. Rashtrakuta sculptures often emphasize the beauty and grace of female forms.

Basalt Rocks

Like other places, the ancient builders at Ellora mainly chose the fine-grained formations of the Deccan trap, ideal for sculpting and rock cutting. In addition to this, the ancient builders also traced the horizontal and vertical joints in the rock formation to minimize labor and time during excavation and rock splitting.

Elephanta and Ellora's rock-cut structures are entirely from Basalt rocks. Basalt is a dark-colored, hard, and fine-grained rock made up entirely of the cooling of Deccan basalt volcanic eruptions and a common rock type in the Earth's crust.

During the volcanic eruptions some 65 million years back, lava flowed during different periods, giving rise to extensive horizontal flows alternating with vesicular trap beds flowing endogenously. These traps retain the heat, travel long distances from the eruptive vent, and cool at the Earth's surface rapidly. They generate patterns of cracking due to thermal shrinkage. The lava lobe swells(inflates) and continues to be supplied lifts in the upper crust. The different lava flows also gave rise to vertical and horizontal joints in the rock formation. Depending upon the nature and mineralogical content of the lava flow, the rock formations also varied in character and texture, giving rise to various qualities like coarse-grained, and fine-grained formations. Though basalt is harder than Granite rocks, cutting the rock or carve sculptures is easier to handle, as they are soft during the initial excavation and harden on exposure to the environment.

The Elephanta Caves monument in Deccan basalt is relatively small in size while the basalt rock at Ellora is a huge monolithic rock. However, both combine significant archaeological, historical, and artistic delights with religious importance. They are both volcanic Geo heritage monuments.

4.A: Gangadhara panel at Cave 1 of Elephanta

The most famous sculpture of Trimurti Shiva at Elephanta is flanked on its left by Ardhanarisvara (a half-Shiva, half-Parvati composite) and Gangadhara legend to its right. (Fig.31).The Gangadhara image to the right of the Trimurti is 4 m (13 ft) wide and 5.207 m (17.08 ft) high, with a theme of Shiva bringing the Ganga River to earth.

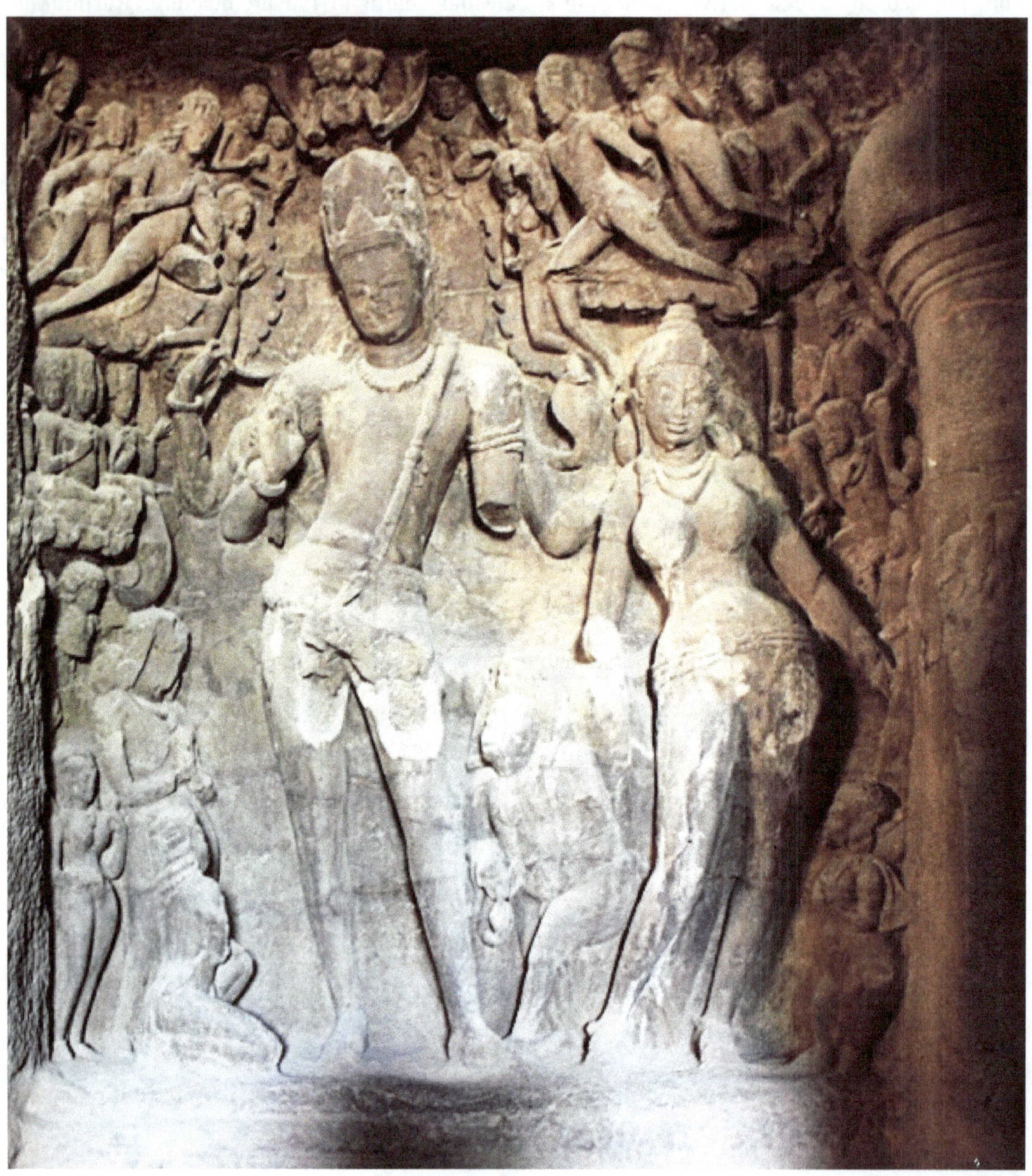

Fig. 31: Gangadhara Panel at Cave 1 of Elephanta

This figure of Gangadhara is one of the notable figures found in the Elephanta Caves. Gangadhara epitomizes Lord Shiva, which means "Bearer of the Ganga River.

The most distinctive feature of the Gangadhara figure is the presence of the river Ganga (Ganga) flowing from Shiva's matted hair. The Elephanta Caves date back to the 5th to 8th centuries CE These caves serve as a significant testament to the architectural and artistic achievements of ancient India. The architectural style of the Elephanta Caves can be classified as a blend of rock-cut architecture and Gupta architecture. Gupta architecture was prevalent even during the 6th Cen CE. Which was characterized by intricate carvings, exquisite sculptures, and well-proportioned structures. This style is evident in the Elephanta Caves' overall design and ornamentation.

This figure represents the iconic moment when Lord Shiva, as Gangadhara, received the mighty Ganga River onto his head to prevent it from flooding the earth. It symbolizes Shiva's ability to control and manage the destructive forces of nature and his association with water and purity.

The panel has Shiva and Parvati as central figures in a standing posture, while Bhagiratha is in a dwarf form to the left of Parvati figure in a standing posture praying to lord Shiva.

The panel is also adorned with many sculptures of celestial beings, such as Brahma, Indra, Vishnu, Varuna, their consorts, Gandharvas, Apsaras, Kinnaras, and Vidhyadharas. These figures are shown in various poses and engaged in diverse activities, adding a celestial charm to the architecture. Rashtrakuta sculptures often emphasize the beauty and grace of female forms.

The Gangadhara image of Shiva and Parvati is damaged, with broken hands and damage at the thigh region. Analyzing each figure:

Shiva is adorned and bedecked with ornaments and a Kirita Makuta in front of the high matted hair. He is a four-armed figure. Wrapped on one of the arms of Shiva is his iconic coiling serpent, whose hood is seen near his left shoulder. Shiva has stretched a string of his matted hair on both sides. He holds the matted hair in the right backhand in a Kapittha hand gesture. Another back left hand (partly broken) gives the semblance of Shiva holding a string of matted hair. Ganga as water droplets are falling on either side of the hair. The front right hand shows Abhaya mudra of protection and the left front hand (Damaged), could be resting on the Gana's head as only fingers are seen. A damaged ornamented drapery covers his lower torso below the waist.

Parvati. The mother goddess Parvati, in a smiling face stands tall to the left of Shiva. She is with a coiffured hair dress and adorned with karanda makuta. The figure is slim, very graceful, and youthful form. The right hand is damaged and appears to be holding a flower.

A Gana figure is between them (stout and dwarf figure), expressing anxiety and panic about whether Shiva can contain the mighty river goddess in his hair.

Ganga is seen above the crown of Shiva, in a cup-like structure in a triple-headed female figure (with broken arms but suggests they were in Anjali mudra)) to depict the three rivers.

Shiva brings the river Ganga down from the heavens to serve man. The Celestial River Ganga's immense power and force while descending from heaven is contained effortlessly in Shiva's hair. The artists have carved a small composite figure of a three-headed goddess up high, a representation of Ganga with the two turbulent headstreams Bhagirathi and Alakananda. Behind the figure of Ganga are the depiction of clouds to suggest the celestial zone (Fig. 32I).

All Gods and flying Gandharvas are depicted surrounding the central image, gathered to watch the descent of a celestial river to earth as a source of abundant water. The gods are identifiable from the vahana (vehicle).

Brahma, Fig. 32A (to the right of Shiva near chest region) is seated on a lotus.

Indra, **Fig. 32A** is next to Brahma on his Airavata elephant.

Vishnu, Fig. 32B, (left of Parvati) is seated on the Garuda.The snake garland around Garuda's neck needs to be noticed. Garuda is in a personified form carrying Vishnu on his shoulders.

Varuna, Fig. 32C, is seen above Brahma and Indra figures like a flying God. He holds a big fish in his hand as his symbol, and his consort Varunani is next to him.

The flying Gandharva, Fig. 32D, with his consort Apsara is well adorned and graceful. Vidyadharas, are like Gandharvas who the attendants of Shiva.

Sadhyas, the ancient master sages, Fig. 32E, has long ears, symbolizing a merited state.

The pitrus, Fig. 32F, as a couple with a bearded face.

Bhagiratha, Fig. 32G, is on the lower side to the left of Parvati figure. He is represented as the heroic mythical king in saintly attire and holding Namaskara mudra. He performed austerities for an extended period to bring the river to liberate his dead Pitrus (Forefathers from the curse of sage

Kapila). They could get Moksha only when the celestial river flowed on their ash mound. his earthly kingdom. Bhagirata also intended to make Ganga flow on land as she brought prosperity to the land.

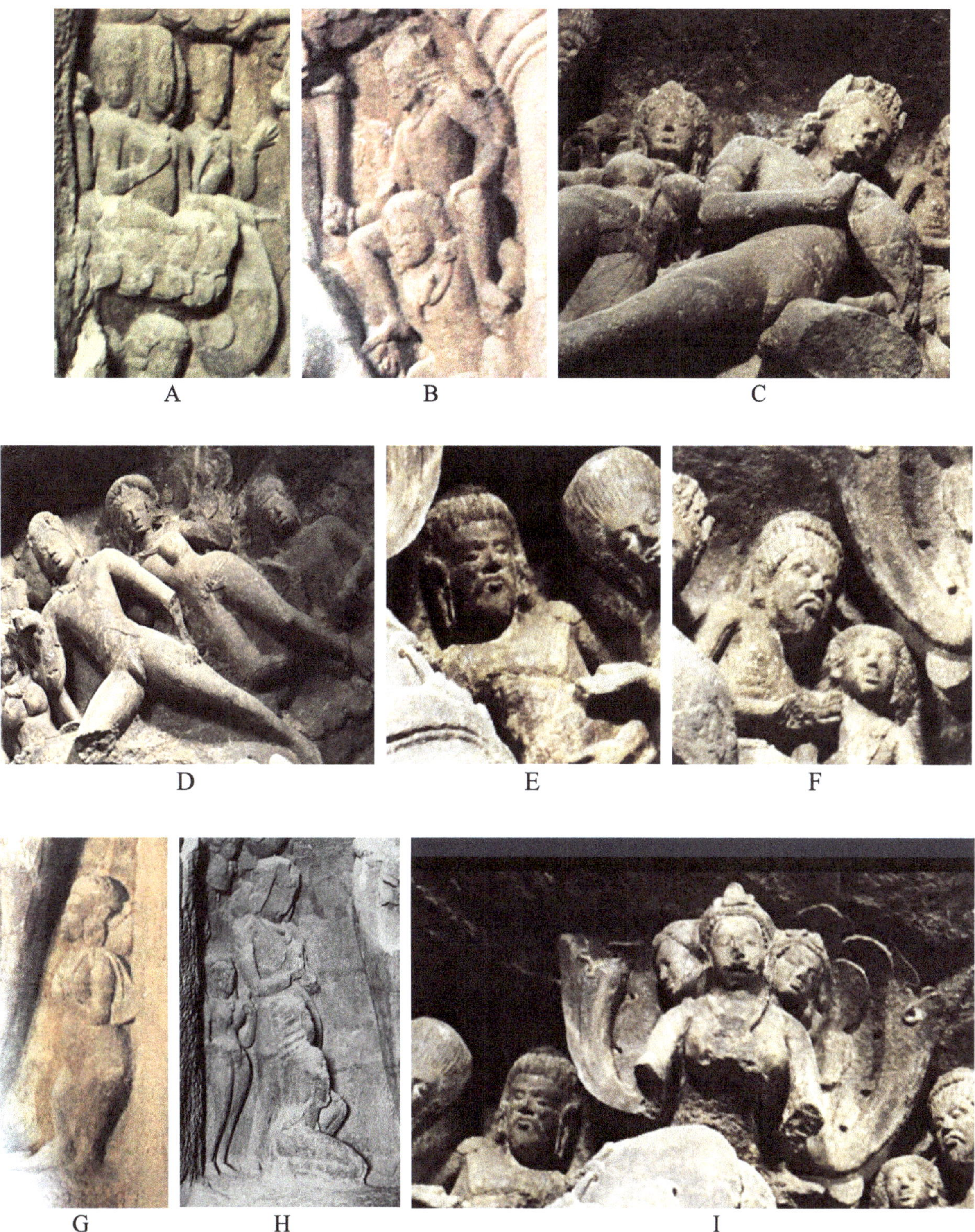

Fig. 32 (A- I): Figures around the central figure of Shiva

Saraswati, Lakshmi,and Indrani, Fig. 32H, are at the base. The tall figure could be Lakshmi, holding a flower. Sarasvati is by the side of Lakshmi. Her hands are broken, but the right-hand position is like it is plucking the strings of Veena. The seated figure could be Indrani, kneeling as a devout figure.

Adi Shankaracharya in Gangastaks quotes about Ganga and the celestial women.

"Gange trilokya sare sakala sura vadhoodhowtha vistheerna thoye," meaning -Hey Ganga, you are most important in all the three worlds, who is so vast and extensive that all women of heaven dip and bathe in you.

Ganga, Fig. 32 I, Ganga is depicted amidst clouds with the headstream tributaries Bhagirati and Alakananda, all three in the personified form of goddesses.

All gods and semi-divine flying gods with curious expressions on their faces wait to witness the great event of the descent of Ganga.

4.B: Kailasa temple of Ellora - Cave 16

There are 34 caves in Ellora. The Rashtrakuta and Kalachuri dynasties built the Hindu caves, and the Yadava rulers built some of the Jaina caves.

Kailasa Temple was built from a rock that was 164 feet deep, 109 feet wide, and 98 feet high. Apart from its size, the rock-cut cave temple stands out for its detailed architecture and sculptures of Hindu deities.

Most of the deities at the left of the entrance are Shaivaite (affiliated with Shiva) figures. The Gangadhara panel at the Ellora Cave 16 uniquely portrays Lord Shiva's power and role in Hindu mythology. The Ellora sculptures reflect the splendid rock-cut architecture of Rashtrakuta king Krishna 1, which is acclaimed as the most spectacular rock-cut monument in the world. The Kailasa Temple was created through a single substantial volcanic basaltic cliff rock. The excavation was from top down, 100 feet deep into the rock. Excavating a monolithic temple would require less labor than moving huge stones to construct a new temple of the same scale. Some academics think that it was built over the reigns of several monarchs. The influence of the Pallava and Chalukya styles can be seen in the temple architecture.

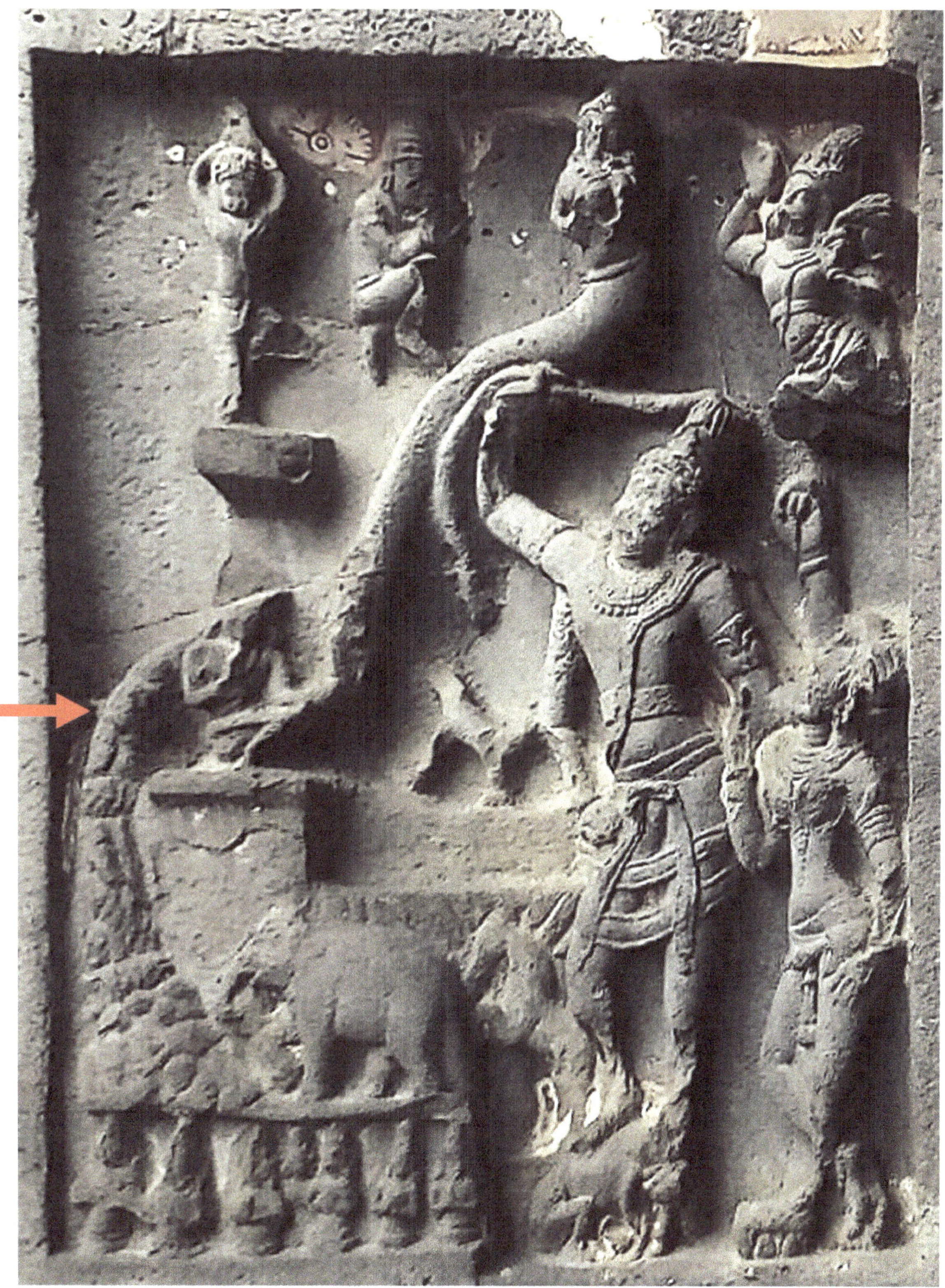

Fig. 33: The Panel of Gangavatarana in Ellora Cave 16

The Panel of Gangavatarana looks different in the Ellora Cave 16, compared to the representation in other temples. Ganga is represented as a single goddess and not with her head stream figures, as seen in other temples that are discussed already. She is flowing like a long tunnel cascading from the top. Shiva has stretched his jata on both sides to arrest the flow.

Shiva is a tall figure with only two arms. He Shows Jatamakuta as headdress and adorned with all ornaments. He has stretched his matted hair on both sides. He wears a short costume and is tied with a robe around the waist.

Parvati is a well-adorned graceful figure standing in a swastika pada, meaning a cross-legged posture. Her left arm is in Katyavalambita mudra and holds a flower in her right hand. The head posture indicates she is looking up at the descent of Ganga.

Ganga figure is a bit damaged but shows Namaskara in hands. The upper part of the body in personified form and the lower part is a flow of water.

Bhagiratha is placed on a stone pedestal on top and depicts a meditation posture in Ekapadasana and hands raised above the head.

Vidyadhara and Gandharva figures are on top as single representations without consorts.

Sage Jahnu: Sage Jahnu appears in the legend of Ganga and Bhagiratha. Ganga river is also known as Jahnavi, meaning the daughter of Jahnu.

Sage Jahunu is depicted below the figure of Bhagirata (marked with an arrow). The legend is, Ganga after her descent, gets locked up in Shiva's matted hair. At the request of Bhagirata, the water gets released. Her torrential waters wreaked havoc upon sage Jahnu's fields and penance. Angered by this, the great sage drank all the Ganga waters to punish her. Seeing this, the devas prayed to the sage to release Ganga, so that she could proceed on her mission to release the souls of the ancestors of Bhagiratha. On the prayers of Bhagirata, the sage Jahnu releases Ganga through his ear. Because Ganga comes out of the ear of sage Jahnu, she was also called Jahnavi. She then flows through the ashes of Bagirata's forefathers, and they were liberated. Sage Jahnu is depicted seated on a pedestal and Ganga is flowing through his ear. Her flow is depicted on the ash mounds.

Animals, like an elephant and a horse (Signifying the mighty and fast-flowing aspects) are rushing to witness the flow of Ganga.

Below the elephant and horse are seven figures which are difficult to identify. Since it is below the earth zone represented by animals, it could be the Nagas of underground welcoming Ganga.

5. Gangavatarana in the Chola Style at Gangai Konda Cholapuram

The Cholas ruled Kanchi from 10th to 13th c. CE. The Chola dynasty, renowned for its patronage of art and architecture, developed its unique sculptural art style, often referred to as the "Chola style." Cholas were Brahmanical Hindus and were devoted to the worship of Shiva. Temples built by the kings of the Chola dynasty between the 11th and 12th centuries in southern India are known for their outstanding art and architecture. Chola art is known for its exquisite craftsmanship, intricate details, elaborate iconographic representations, attention to detail, and graceful yet powerful depictions of deities and celestial beings. Sculptures depict graceful postures and are also known for fluid and Dynamic Poses in beautiful expressions.

Rajendra Chola-I (1012-1044 A.D) son of the Great Rajaraja-I, established this Gangai Konda Cholapuram temple at their capital after his grand victorious march to river Ganga in Northern India. He assumed the title of Rajendra during his coronation and continued to rule along with his father Rajaraja-I for a while.

Two panels with the theme of Gangadhara figures are presented here:

- Panel 1 is from Gangai Konda Cholapuram temple.
- Panel 2 is now preserved in the art gallery of Tanjavur Palace Museum.

Description of Panel 1

Panel 1 is from Gangai Konda Cholapuram in Tamil Nadu which has a figure of Gangadhara on the side frames.

Gangadhara Shiva- a four-armed standing figure of Shiva embracing Parvati, stands by his side. Shiva has stretched the matted hair on the right side with the back right hand. In a personified form, Ganga is depicted seated in his jata, holding Anjali mudra. She is shown cascading down from his hair. His back left hand also holds the string of matted hair.

The lower right hand is gently placed on the breast of Parvathi. (This signifies that he possesses the shakti of Parvati) and the lower left hand is placed on the waist of Parvati. The upper left part of the panel shows the mriga.

Shiva is in Jatamakuta (Matted locksShiva has spread his jata/ matted hair on the right side to control the force of river Ganga while falling down. Regarding the costumes, Shiva is in a short costume. The decorative and elaborate udarabandha (Waist belt) with pearly decorations adorn his waist. His angavastra the cloth tied on the waist, is depicted on both sides He wears a leg ornament called Kadaga above the ankle region. He shows a high jata makuta, armbands and kadaga on arms also. On the forehead is the third eye.

Both Shiva and Parvati figures are adorned with yajnopavita.

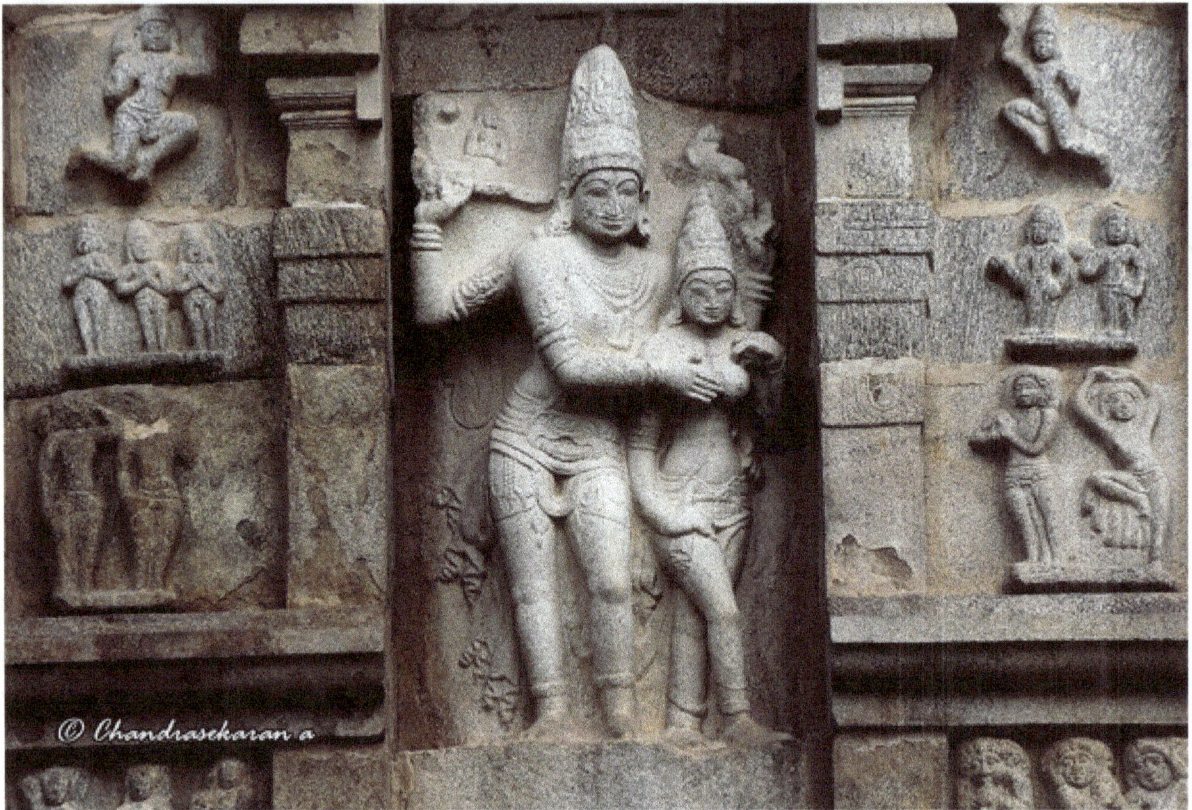

Fig. 34: Panel 1 in Gangaikonda Cholapuram temple, Tamil Nadu

Parvati is adorned in a long costume with all ornaments and a karanda makuta on her head. (A layered conical headdress or crown). She shows the right arm in katyavalambita mudra on the right thigh while the left is placed above the breast. Eyes are looking down, indicative of her readiness to move forward. Parvati depicts the legs in a running away posture in Baddha Swastika, indicating her fear of looking at the fall of Ganga. The fear of Parvati is a pictorial representation of how she was scared. Shiva is trying to console Parvati's fear as Ganga will be Trilochana jata vasini (GS.19), meaning one who resides in Shiva's matted hair, and all the force of her fall is controlled by his jata. He is consoling Parvati that it is essential to let Ganga flow in a channelized form because Ganaga is *Nitya suddha*, and *punyayai* (GS.28, GS.87) meaning ever pure and auspicious. The right arm of the Devi is placed on the thigh.

Gangadevi in a personified form holds Anjali mudra in hands as a mark of devotion to Shiva.

62

The figures of mriga, a deer, and Ganga are in the same plane. This is a metaphoric comparison to the speed associated with Ganga and the deer. Ganga is called *Shigragha* (GS.53) meaning one who moves with speed and force.

Figures on the frame

On either side of Panel 1 are small figures in four rows. The top row on both sides shows flying Vidyadharas, who are attendants of Shiva. The middle row of figures is Sadhyas. They are depicted as peaceful old people with jatamakuta on their heads and Yajnopavita. Sadhyas are a particular class of celestial beings, the accomplished deity of mantras. The bottom row of figures is the Gandharvas and Apsara couple. Apsara is depicted in a dancing posture.The fourth bottom row of figures is the Shivaganas.

Description of Panel 2

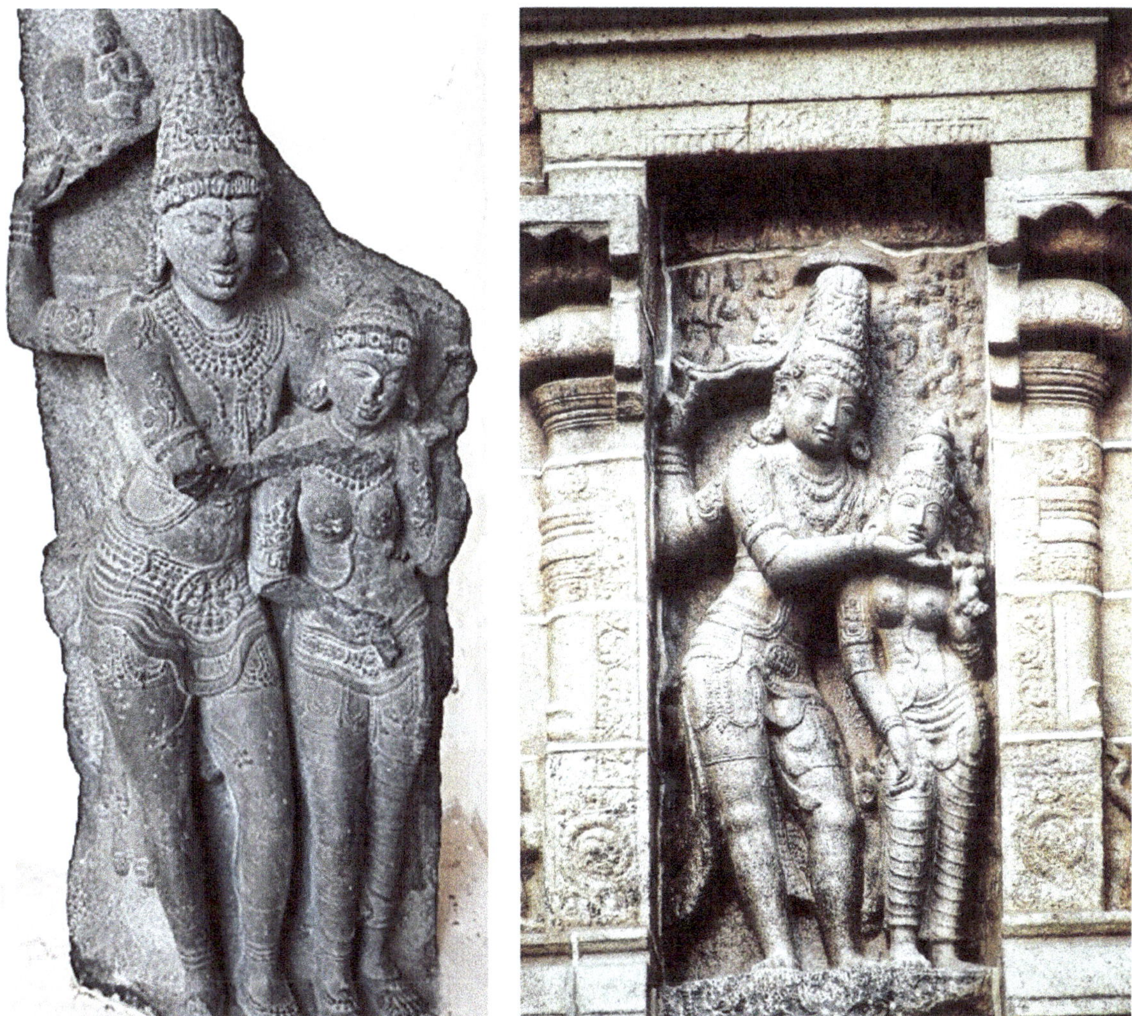

Fig. 35 A (Left) and B (Right): Two Depictions of Gangadhara Sculpture from Tamil Nadu

Gangadhara Shiva Penel depicts only three figures, Shiva, Parvati, and Ganga. Figures are beautifully carved in probably granite stone.

Shiva is well adorned with ornaments, and a short costume, and is four-armed without holding any accessories. He is three-eyed, wears a high Jatamakuta, and the string of his matted hair is stretched from his top right and left hand. Ganga is seated with folded hands in Namaskara mudra on his right side. He holds Parvati in his front hands and looks like he is trying to console Parvati.

Parvati is slim graceful, and two armed. She is a well-adorned figure wearing a long costume. Her headdress is in Karanda makuta. She looks down showing a scared expression to witness the force of the fall of Ganga. Shiva is trying to give her assurance of safety.

6. Reverence of Ganga as a Mighty River: Har Har Gange

Ganga, the mighty river is worshipped by millions of Hindus as she is believed to be a spiritual liberator .Ganga's significance has been celebrated in various forms of literature, arts, music, Poems, and songs. Artworks highlighting the river's spiritual and cultural significance have been created centuries ago. In Tirthayatra Parva, before the great war, the epic states

"the one who observes firm [ethical] vows, having bathed at Prayaga during Magha, O best of the Bharatas, becomes spotless and reaches heaven."

The socio-religious rituals associated with the Ganga unravel the cultural heritage interwoven with the Ganga. India has been observing the vibrant festivals that pay homage to the river. Throngs of devotees gather to offer prayers, light candles, and release flower-laden offerings onto its sacred waters. From the grand celebrations of Ganga Maha-aarti to the sacred dip in the river during Kumbh Mela, a gathering of millions seeking spiritual salvation enjoy the joyous festivals and celebrations. The rituals associated with Ganga are well detailed in ancient scriptures.

Rigveda Mandala 10.30.2 says *"Go to the reservoir O Adhvaryus, worship the waters, child with your oblations."*

The Adhvaryu priests (Yajurveda priests who perform the manual part of a ritual). Are depicted in the rock of Mahabalipuram (Fig. 25) to be worshipping the river in the rituals and waving a light in reverence at dawn and dusk religious rituals.

Adi Shankaracharya in Gangashtaka quotes *"Sayam prathar muneenaam kusa kusuma chayai"*

Meaning saints were giving the dawn and dusk salutations with water full of floating grass and flowers.

These traditional rituals prescribed in the scriptures insist that religious rituals are to be performed on the river Ganga at dawn and dusk. This practice is meticulously followed by Hindus even to this day. People continue to offer prayers, flowers, and lamps to the river, expressing their devotion and seeking blessings.

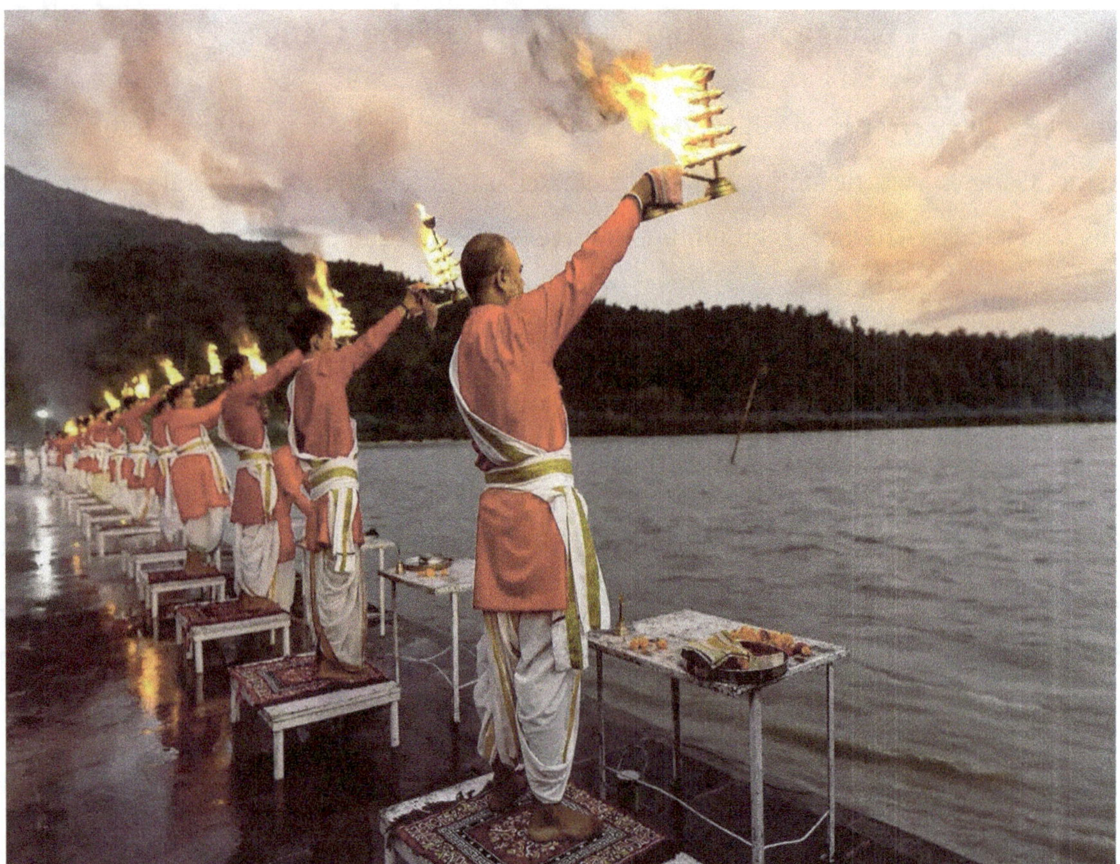

Fig. 36: Ganga aarti ritual performed at dawn by priests at the riverbank in Varanasi, India

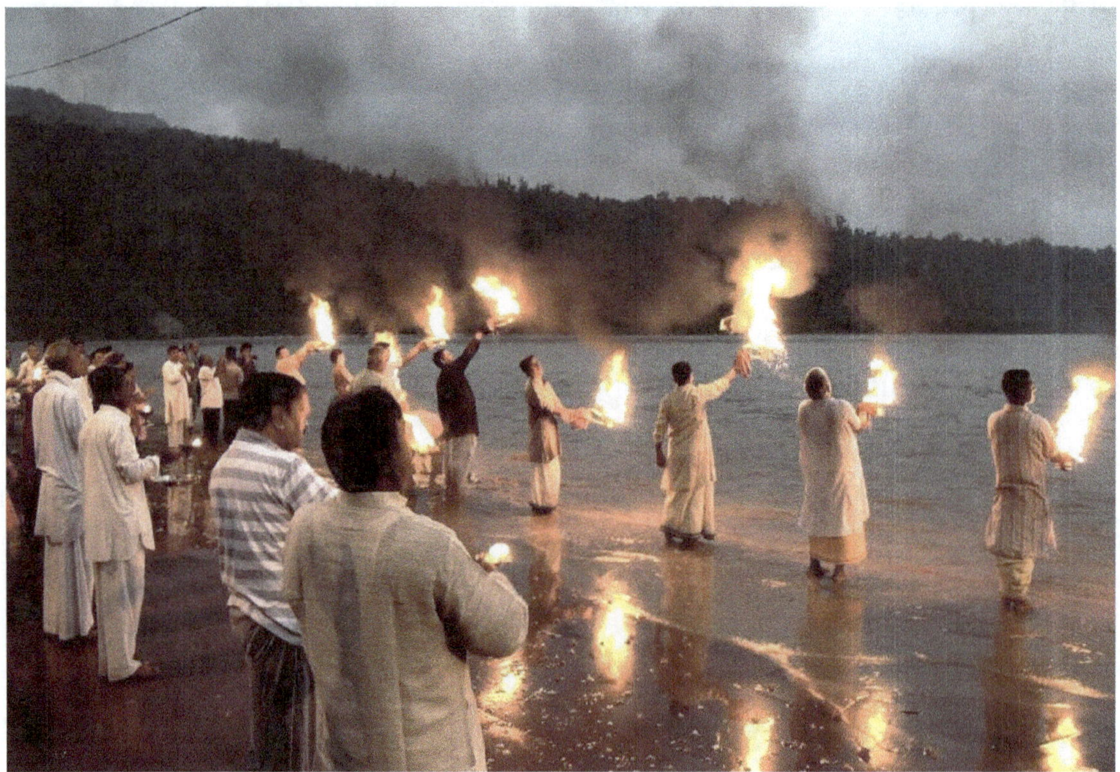

Fig. 37: Ganga aarti ceremonial ritual performed by priests at the Triveni Ghat, Rishikesh

Maha Ganga aarti ceremony ritual performed by priests at Triveni Ghat at Rishikesh at dusk time goes to this day with rhythmic chanting of hymns, creating a spiritual ambiance with light and sound vibrations. Triveni Ghat is a famous pilgrimage with colorful decorations during festivals like Deepavali, Sankrant, and full moon days. The atmosphere resonates with devotion and reverence to the goddess Ganga.

Hindus consider The Ganga a sacred river. It is believed to have purifying and cleansing properties. Many Hindu rituals like marriages, funerals, and other religious rites involve using Ganga water for purification and consecration purposes. The Ganga and its banks are associated with several important pilgrimage sites. Cities like Varanasi (also known as Kashi) and Haridwar have continued to attract pilgrims from all over India and beyond. These sites are believed to have unique spiritual energy due to their proximity to the Ganga.

The Mahabharata mentions a bathing pilgrimage at Prayag to *prayaschitta* (atonement, penance) for past mistakes and guilt. Ganga is *Sarasvati Samyukta* (GS.8) meaning meeting Sarasvati at Allahabad. She is praised as *prayaganilayayai namah* (GS.77). There are other references to Prayaga and river-side festivals in ancient Indian texts, including where present-day Kumbh Melas are held.

Many Hindus travel to the river to participate in rituals, prayers, and ceremonies. Bathing in the Ganga is believed to wash away sins and bring spiritual purity. Festivals such as Kumbh Mela are one of the largest religious gatherings in the world. People gather to take a holy dip in the river and seek her blessings.

Allahabad - Prayagraj is a holy place for the bathing ceremony at Sunset at the confluence of Ganga, Yamuna and Sarasvati rivers. During Kumbh Mela, a mass of Hindu pilgrimage of faith gather to bathe in a sacred or holy river. Bathing is thought to cleanse a person of all their sins.

This is a leading festival site located at Allahabad on the banks of the confluence of the three rivers.

Hindus' deep spiritual and cultural connection with the river Ganga in India is a continued tradition of at least 5,000 years. Despite the changes over the centuries, the Ganga's role as a symbol of purity, divinity, and cultural heritage has remained steadfast in the hearts and minds of the Indian people.

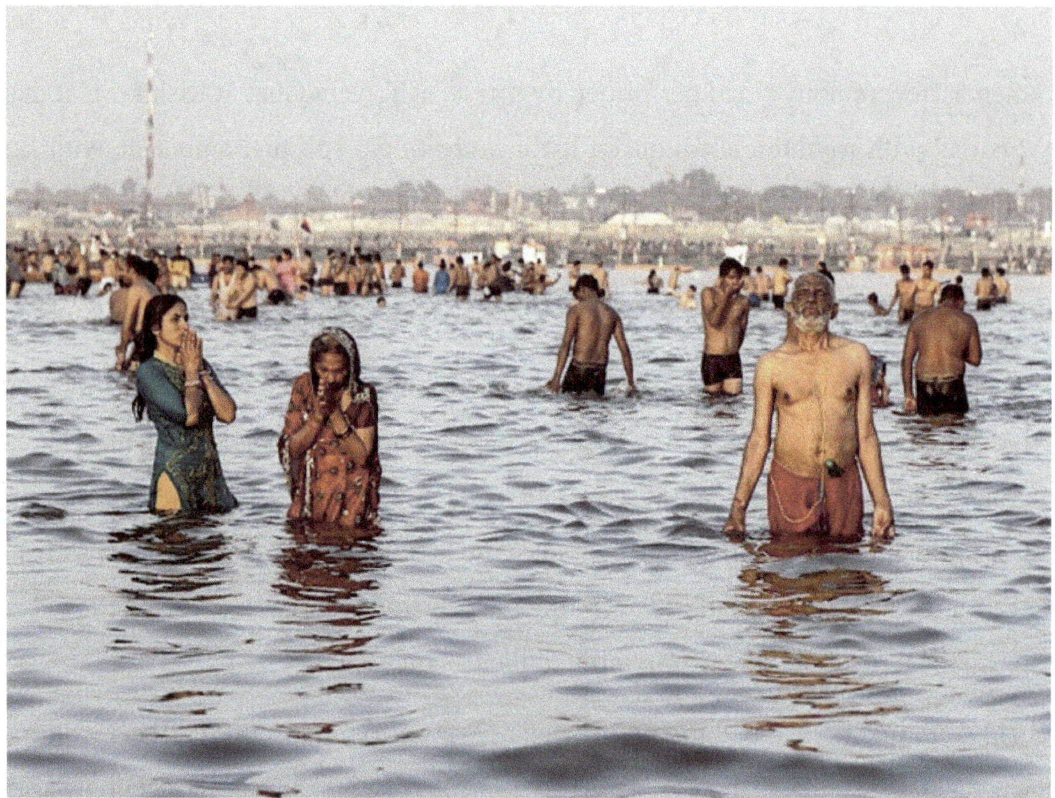

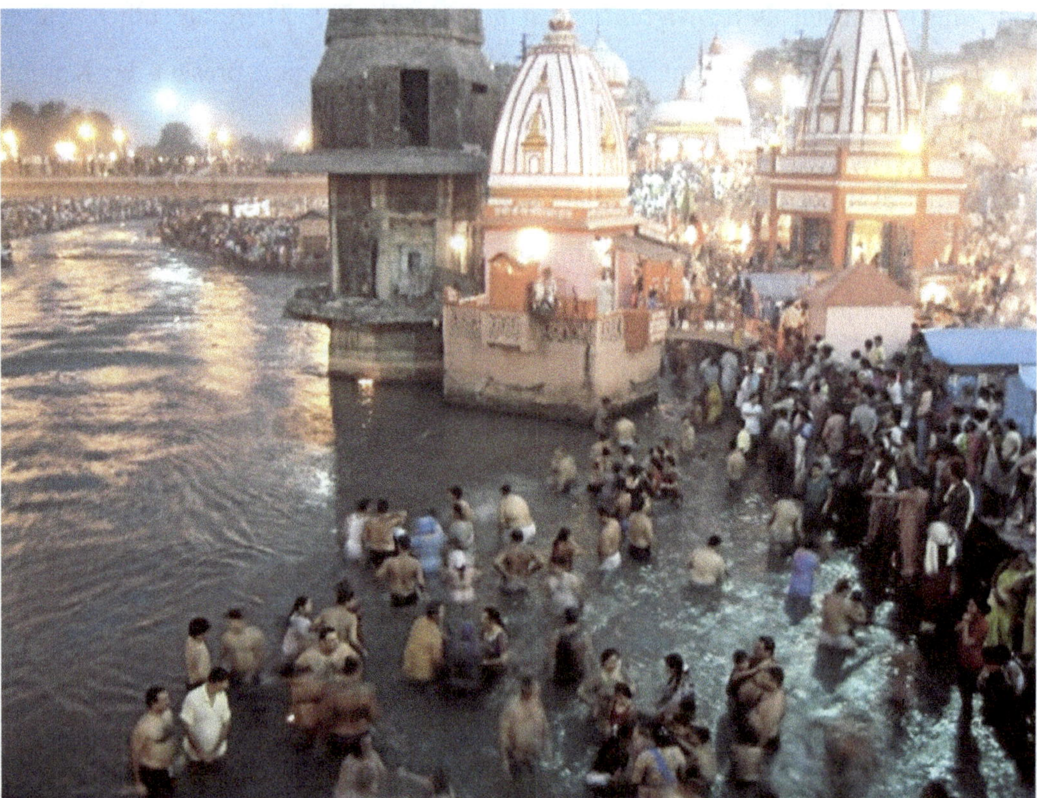

Fig. 38 (Top) and 39 (Bottom): The sacred dip at Ganga during the Kumbhamela celebrations

7. Conclusion

For thousands of years, the Ganga (affectionately known as Ganga ma) has flowed through the hearts and souls of millions, weaving a tapestry of reverence, spirituality, and renewal. The tale of Bhagiratha's devotion, determination, and successful endeavor to bring the celestial Ganga to Earth is often cited as an example of "Bhagirata Prayatna". His efforts to fulfill the righteous dual goals of achieving moksha to his forefathers and helping the living creatures in society with purified water are like a moral lesson to mankind. The episode of Bhagirata's efforts reinforces and boosts the moral that the outcome of sincere efforts is always fruitful.

The Descent of the Ganga, a significant event in Hindu mythology, is brought out in many temples of India, but the rock relief carvings at Mahabalipuram provide a panoramic visual representation of the glory of the Descent of Ganga. It is an artistic marvel holding great architectural heritage the cultural and religious significance. These magnificent structures are enduring examples of India's, attracting tourists and scholars worldwide.

The concept of "*Vasudhaiva Kutumbakam*", visualizing and experiencing harmony with all individuals and living creatures, promoting peace, tolerance, and ecological coexistence, is well brought out in the rock relief. It emphasizes the need for mutual respect and the importance of preserving nature for the betterment of the world.

As we immerse ourselves in the topic of the Ganga, it becomes evident that the Ganga is much more than a mere river. It is a testament to the enduring spirit of a nation, an embodiment of faith and devotion, and a symbol of eternal renewal.

8. Appendix: Ganga Ashtottara Shatanamavali, English Lyrics

Om gamgayai namah | Om visnupadasambhutayai namah | Om haravallabhayai namah | Om himacalendratanayayai namah | Om girimandalagaminyai namah | Om tarakaratijananyai namah | Om sagaratmajatarakayai namah | Om sarasvatīsamayuktayai namah | Om sughosayai namah | Om sindhugaminyai namah | 10 |

Om bhagīratyai namah | Om bhagyavatyai namah | Om bhagīratarathanugayai namah | Om trivikramapadodbhutayai namah | Om trilokapathagaminyai namah | Om ksīrasubhrayai namah | Om bahuksīrayai namah | Om ksīravrksasamakulayai namah | Om trilocanajatavasayai namah | Om rnatrayavimocinyai namah | 20 |

Om tripurarisirahcudayai namah | Om jahnavyai namah | Om narakabhītihrte namah | Om avyayayai namah | Om nayananandadayinyai namah | Om nagaputrikayai namah | Om niranjanayai namah | Om nityasuddhayai namah | Om nīrajalipariskrtayai namah |

Om savitryai namah | 30 |

Om salilavasayai namah | Om sagarambusamedhinyai namah | Om ramyayai namah | Om bindusarase namah | Om avyaktayai namah | Om avyaktarupadhrte namah | Om umasapatnyai namah | Om subhrangayai namah | Om srīmatyai namah | Om dhavalambarayai namah | 40 |

Om akhandalavanavasayai namah | Om kamthendukrtasekarayai namah | Om amrtakarasalilayai namah | Om līlalimgitaparvatayai namah | Om virincikalasavasayai namah | Om trivenyai namah | Om trigunatmakayai namah | Om samgata aghaughasamanyai namah | Om bhītihartre namah |

Om samkhadumdubhinisvanayai namah | 50 |

Om bhagyadayinyai namah | Om nandinyai namah | Om sīghragayai namah |

Om saranyai namah | Om sasisekarayai namah | Om saṅkaryai namah | Om sapharīpurnayai namah | Om bhargamurdhakrtalayayai namah | Om bhavapriyayai namah | 60 |

Om satyasandhapriyayai namah | Om hamsasvarupinyai namah | Om bhagīratabhrtayai namah |

Om anantayai namah | Om saraccandranibhananayai namah | Om omkararupinyai namah |

Om analayai namah | Om krīdakallolakarinyai namah | Om svargasopanasaranyai namah |

Om sarvadevasvarupinyai namah | 70 |

Om ambahpradayai namah | Om duhkhahantryainamah | Om santisantanakarinyai namah |

Om daridryahantryai namah | Om sivadayai namah | Om samsaravisanasinyai namah | Om prayaganilayayai namah | Om srīdayai namah | Om tapatrayavimocinyai namah |

Om saranagatadīnartaparitranayai namah | 80 |

Om sumuktidayai namah | Om papahantryai namah | Om pavanaṅgayai namah | Om parabrahmasvarupinyai namah | Om purnayai namah | Om puratanayai namah | Om punyayai namah | Om punyadayai namah | Om punyavahinyai namah | Om pulomajarcitayai namah | 90 |

Om bhudayai namah | Om putatribhuvanayai namah | Om jayayai namah | Om jamgamayai namah | Om jamgamadharayai namah | Om jalarupayai namah | Om jagaddhatryai namah |

Om jagadbhutayai namah | Om janarcitayai namah | Om jahnuputryai namah | 100 |

Om jaganmatre namah | Om jambhudvīpaviharinyai namah | Om bhavapatnyai namah |

Om bhīsmamatre namah | Om siktayai namah | Om ramyarupadhrte namah | Om umasahodaryai namah | Om ajnanatimirapahrte namah | 108 |

|| Om tatsat || || srī gamgastottara satanamavalih sampurna ||

9. References

1. 108 Names Goddess Ganga, Rudra Centre Living Enlightenment, https://www.rudraksha-ratna.com/articles/108-names-goddess-ganga

2. 108 Names of Ganga - Ganga Ashtottara Shatanamavali Lyrics in English, Temples in India Info, https://templesinindiainfo.com/108-names-of-ganga-ganga-ashtottara-shatanamavali-lyrics-in-english/

3. Maa Ganga Stortam, Bhakti Bharat, https://www.bhaktibharat.com/mantra/maa-ganga-stortam

4. Descent of the Ganges (Mahabalipuram), Wikipedia, https://en.wikipedia.org/wiki/Descent_of_the_Ganges_(Mahabalipuram)#

5. Singhal Shweta, Mahabalipuram Monuments: Ancient stories carved in stone, July 2018, https://zestinatote.com/places-to-visit-mahabalipuram/

6. Info on Five Rathas – Mahabalipuram, Wikipedia, https://upload.wikimedia.org/wikipedia/commons/e/ed/Info_Five_Rathas_Mahabalipuram_Sep22_A7C_02536.jpg

7. Ganges River Basin, National Geographic Education, https://education.nationalgeographic.org/resource/ganges-river-basin/

8. Josh Jagran, Why is it believed that the River Ganga is self-cleaning?, Mar 2018, https://www.jagranjosh.com/general-knowledge/why-is-it-believed-that-the-river-ganga-is-self-cleaning-1520601151-1

9. Fosmire Edward, The Great Relief at Mamallapuram, Course: Art of Asia Unit 7, Khan Academy, https://www.khanacademy.org/humanities/art-asia/south-asia/x97ec695a:500-1100-c-e-deccan-and-south/a/the-great-relief-at-mamallapuram

10. Gonsavles Timothy A, Practise Panel Lighthouse Mahabalipuram, Wikimedia Commons, Sep 2022, https://commons.wikimedia.org/wiki/File:Practise_Panel_Lighthouse_Mahabalipuram_Sep22_A7C_02532.jpg

11. Gatha Moni, Kailasanathar in Kanchipuram/ Kanchi- A Pallava marvel in stucco and sandstone, Mar 2019, https://monidipa.net/2019/03/15/kailashnathar-in-kanchipuram-a-pallava-marvel-in-stucco-and-sandstone/

12. Elephanta Gandhara, Wikimedia Commons, https://commons.wikimedia.org/wiki/File:Elephanta_Gangadhara.JPG

13. Sheth Hetu et. al, The volcanic geoheritage of the Elephanta Caves, Deccan Traps, western India, Geoheritage 9(3):359-372, https://www.researchgate.net/publication/319312553_The_volcanic_geoheritage_of_the_Elephanta_Caves_Deccan_Traps_western_India_2017

14. Ellora Caves, Unesco World Heritage Convention, https://whc.unesco.org/en/list/243/

15. Elephanta Caves – Gangadhara, Wikimedia Commons, https://upload.wikimedia.org/wikipedia/commons/9/93/Elephanta_Caves_Gangadhara.jpg

16. Gangadhara Panels at Elephanta Caves, Mar 2018, https://www.flickr.com/photos/86172199@N04/40533868762/in/photostream/

17. Gangadhara, Chola period, 9th - 10th centuries, Stone sculpture, Thanjavur Palace Museum, Wikimedia Commons, https://commons.wikimedia.org/wiki/File:Gangadhara,_Chola_period,_9th_-_10th_centuries,_Stone_sculpture,_Thanjavur_Palace_Museum.jpg

18. Arumugam Chandrasekaran, Gangadhara (Siva) with Devi, Gangai Konda Cholapuram Series 13, Mar 2015, https://www.flickr.com/photos/29848963@N03/16667752216

19. Ganga Aarti in Varanasi, Times Now, Mar 2022, https://www.timesnowhindi.com/varanasi/article/ganga-aarti-will-conduct-in-villages-on-tha-bank-of-river/404888

20. Fig.4 and Fig. 18 courtesy of Jayen Mistry and Rasik Mistry.

21. Fig. 29 courtesy of Gautam Subbarao.

10. About the Author

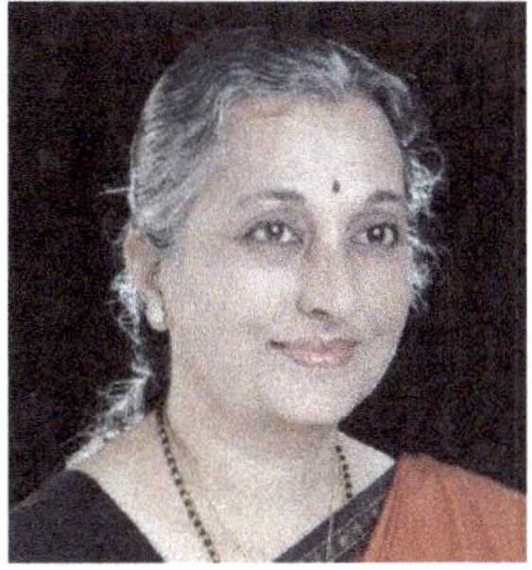 Rekha Rao, a master's degree holder in Indology from University of Mysore, is also an accomplished classical dancer. In the year 2000, she took up independent research work in Indology under the guidance of Dr.S.R. Rao, Former Deputy Director General, Archaeological survey of India, and since 2010, on her own. Her interests in the temple sculptures have made her visit and study various temples in India focusing on the sculptures of apsaras, Buddhist architecture and Indus Seals.

Books by the same Author

Amazon.com author page: www.amazon.com/author/rekharao

1. Erotic Sculptures in Indian Temples: A New Perspective, Available online on Amazon in both eBook and print book format: https://a.co/d/fBWrcTK

2. Symbolography in Indus seals, Available online on Amazon in both eBook and print book format: https://www.amazon.in/Symbolography-Indus-Seals-Rekha-Rao-ebook/dp/B016QQKBQE

3. Buddhism in Rani Ki Vav, Patan - A World Heritage Monument, Sold by Amazon Digital Services, Inc, ASIN: B00Y6UXHPK. Available online on Amazon: http://amzn.to/2dGc9WG

4. Rani Ki Vav – The Abode of Bodhisattva and Dakinis, Published by Aditya Prakashan, New Delhi, 2014, ISBN: 9788177421354

5.. Vajrayana Buddhism in Khajuraho Sculptures, Published by Power Publishers, 2012, ISBN – 978-93-82070-02-3, ISBN – 93-82070-02-3

6. Science and Golden Ratios in Mandala Architecture, Published by D.K Printworld (P) Ltd., 2011, ISBN – 81-246-0587-4, ISBN – 978-81-246-0587-5

7. Apsaras in Hoysala art - A new dimension, Published by Aryan Books International, 2009, ISBN- 978-81-7305-379-5

8.. Therapeutics in Indian sculptures - Ranki vav, Patan, Published by Aryan books international, 2006, 2007, ISBN – 81-7305-312-x, ISBN – 9788173053122

9. . The Depiction of Vedic Priests in Indus Seals, Available online on Amazon in both ebook and print book format: https://www.amazon.com/Depiction-Vedic-Priests-Indus-Seals/dp/1717855202/ref=sr_1_9?ie=UTF8&qid=1537762482&sr=8-9&keywords=Rekha+rao

10. Ancient Vedic Beverages, Available online on Amazon in both ebook and print book format: https://www.amazon.com/gp/product/B082SGXR5H/ref=dbs_a_def_rwt_hsch_vapi_taft_p1_i2

11. The Truth About Aryas, Available online on Amazon in both ebook and print book format: https://www.amazon.com/gp/product/B0835T78SJ/ref=dbs_a_def_rwt_hsch_vapi_taft_p1_i0

12. The Glory of Hoysala Queens: Belur Chennakeshava Temple, Available online on Amazon in both ebook and print book format: https://www.amazon.com/gp/product/B07T8TC7KV/ref=dbs_a_def_rwt_hsch_vapi_taft_p1_i4

13. The Dictionary of Indus Symbols, Available online on Amazon in both ebook and print book format: https://www.amazon.com/gp/product/B07J3WKKC1/ref=dbs_a_def_rwt_hsch_vapi_taft_p1_i1

14. Ayurveda in Indian Temples, Available online on Amazon in both ebook and print book format: https://a.co/d/7zPCCHV